Borderline Personality Disorder

The Comprehensive Guide to Cognitive Behavioral Therapy. Overcoming Depression, Reduce Anxiety, Rewire Your Brain, and Enhance Your Relationships (2022 For Beginners)

Table of Contents

Introduction

*"**Borderline Personality Disorder (BPD)** is a mode defect that affects how people connect with one another. This is the most well-known personality disorder." "*

In general, a person with a personality disorder will behave markedly different from the ordinary person in terms of how he thinks, understands, feels, and interacts with others. Borderline Personality Disorder (BPD) is a mental illness in which emotions are difficult to control. This indicates that persons with BPD feel emotions strongly and for an extended period of time, and it is difficult for them to return to a stable baseline following an emotionally stimulating incident.

This issue may result in unconsciousness, a negative self-image, tumultuous relationships, and extreme emotional reactivity to stresses.

Borderline Personality Issue is a mental health disorder that affects how you think and feels about yourself and others, causing problems in daily living. It involves issues with self-image, difficulties managing emotions and actions, and a history of unstable relationships.

You have a strong fear of solitude or instability if you have Borderline Personality Disorder and you may struggle with being alone.

Even if you desire to have a loving and long-lasting relationship, improper anger, rapid and frequent mood swings might drive others away.

Borderline personality disorder often manifests itself in early adolescence.

The illness is known to worsen throughout puberty and to improve progressively with age. Don't give up if you have a borderline personality disorder. Many persons with this disease improve with therapy and may learn to live a happy life. Borderline Personality Disorder is an illness characterized by fluctuating emotions, self-image, and persistent behavioral patterns.

These symptoms are often the outcome of positive acts as well as troubles in the relationship. Sufferers with Borderline Personality Disorder may endure extreme bouts of rage, despair, and anxiety that may persist for hours or days.

People suffering from BPD are very sensitive. It's been described as having an exposed nerve terminal by some. Small things may have big consequences. And once you're angry, it'll be difficult to settle down.

It is simple to see how emotional oscillations and self-inconvenience cause confusion and disappointment, even in thoughtless action in partnerships.

You may say harsh things or behave in unsafe or improper ways and then feel guilty or humiliated about it. It's a painful loop from which there is no way out. But this is not the case. There are successful BPD treatments and coping methods that may help you feel more in control of your thoughts, emotions, and behaviors.

Typically, it manifests as follows:

▢ Reactions that are inappropriate or too emotional

▢ Extremely emotional behavior

▢ An unsteady relationship history

Acute mood fluctuations, abrupt conduct, and strong emotions may make it difficult for persons with a borderline personality disorder to finish their schooling, hold down solid employment, and sustain long, healthy relationships.

In addition...

Furthermore, Borderline Personality Disorder (BPD) is a mental disease that makes it difficult to feel at ease.

It makes it harder to regulate one's emotions and

movements. It generates complications for other individuals. Furthermore, persons with BPD have a high degree of anxiety and fury and might readily take offense to other people's acts or words. People with BPD may have negative thoughts and beliefs about themselves and others.

This might create problems in their professional, home, and social lives.

Some persons with BPD do themselves damage. People have diverse perspectives on BPD / EUPD, and it may be a contentious diagnosis. But, regardless of how you interpret your experiences and whatever words you like to use (if any), the crucial thing to remember is the feelings and behaviors linked with BPD / EUPD. It is very tough to live with and requires compassion and understanding.

Chapter 1

What Is Borderline Personality Disorder?

This section has been dedicated to providing you with an unambiguous, functionally plausible image of BPD. If you suspect that you or someone close to you may have BPD, it is important to understand what this entails.

Before you begin reading this section, it is critical to understand that you cannot diagnose yourself with BPD. Regardless of whether you learn about some of the symptoms of BPD and think, "That's me!" you should consult with an expert (an analyst, a specialist, or another someone who analyses mental disorders) to determine if you really have BPD.

Trying to diagnose oneself with a mental ailment is similar to trying to diagnose you with cancer or heart disease.

You need an expert to perform it since you almost certainly lack the necessary tools, talents, or goal viewpoint.

Furthermore, if you form an incorrect conclusion, you are unlikely to get proper assistance. I've encountered a few folks who believed they had BPD but turned out to have another illness, such as sadness, bipolar confusion, or posttraumatic stress disorder.

Similarly, since the recommended medications for cancer are not the same as those for cardiac sickness, each mental or emotional problem needs a different therapy. As a result, you'll need to guarantee that your conclusion is exact, and the best method to do so is to consult an expert. As a result, use this part to comprehend what BPD is all about and to demonstrate indicators of the improved grasp of the disorder's negative effects.

BPD, MENTAL DISORDERS, AND PERSONALITY DISORDERS

A personality disorder is simply a consistent example of associating with an environment that does not operate effectively. Furthermore, these illnesses produce excruciating discomfort and may make it difficult to see someone or lead to difficulties in achieving goals in daily life (for example, obtaining or maintaining an optimal activity).

Personality disorders include avoidant, fanatical impulsive, needy, jumpy, schizoid, schizotypal, narcissistic, theatrical, standoffish, and, of course, borderline personality disorder.

Having a personality disorder usually means that you have a slew of other issues that have been bothering you for a long time.

To be found to have a personality disorder, you must be an adult in most cases. Individuals judged to have a personality disorder as adults, on the other hand, will often state that they have fought with these problems for as long as they can remember. As a result, we acknowledge that many people have had these problems since they were children.

Having a personality disorder does not suggest that you have an imperfect personality, a bad personality, or that you are a cruel or unlikeable person. Essentially, the assumption is that people with personality disorders have something in their qualities that causes problems for them and others.

For the time being, we don't quite agree with this, for a variety of reasons.

Second, this word implies that the disease is inside you and that if you could simply repair yourself, everything would be normal. We can't help but disagree with this viewpoint.

There is a lot of evidence that the earth (for example, stress, injury, abuse, and other similar things) plays a significant role in a variety of mental diseases, including personality disorders.

Furthermore, carrying the condition inside you might lead to feelings of humiliation and criticism toward others.

Finally, the term personality disorder implies that if you have a personality disorder, you have always had it (it is a part of your personality, a part of what makes you the person you are), and you will always have it. In any event, as you'll see in Part 4, there is evidence that BPD does not always persist in the way that people believe it does.

As a result, having BPD does not suggest that you have a flawed personality or that you will always struggle with the problems you are experiencing right now.

It simply means that you have an example of thinking, feeling, and doing that may be impeding your ability to live a high-quality life, protect your relationships, or achieve your goals. The fact that the DSM-IV-TR is based on the idea that mental disorders are similar to clinical illnesses or diseases complicates problems. The DSM-IV-TR employs an "infection paradigm" for mental clutters, linking them to a pathology (brokenness) inside the person (or in nature), much like pneumonia, diabetes, or other similar disorders. The problem with this thinking is that mental disease does not seem to act in the same way that ailments do. To begin with, you can't "get" a mental condition like you can pneumonia. Second, unlike diseases such as diabetes, mental clutters have not been linked to any bodily breakdown that may cause them. Third, many of the symptoms of the specified condition (for example, wretchedness) are also seen in a variety of other illnesses, making the distinction between these disarranges hazy. Interestingly, physicians can tell the difference between diabetes and bosom malignant development.

Fourth, consider what you do, think, or feel.

The assumption is that certain things you may do, think, or feel will indicate the proximity of a concealed problem. That is a significant leap to make. Researchers can't go into someone's body or brain and detect a fundamental issue, as they can when they uncover a cancerous tumor. Fifth, the disease model, like the term personality disorder, places the problem primarily inside you. As seen following, if you have BPD, a considerable proportion of the illnesses you deal with are connected with diseases in the world rather than problems that reside inside you. Furthermore, the changes you may need to make in order to be happier may involve altering your personality or changing how you behave, think, or feel. As a result, we agree that what you do, think, and feel is much more important than whether you are confused.

THE HISTORY OF BPD

The widely believed belief was that there were two basic categories of mental diseases or disorders. Despondency was a categorization that includes people who were aware of their surroundings but suffered from passionate illnesses such as melancholy or anxiousness problems.

The second categorization, psychosis, comprised people who had strange thoughts and interactions (for example, visuals) that were not typical, and these patients were ruled to have the illness, for example, schizophrenia.

Patients who did not have illnesses severe enough to be labeled insane (as a result, their thinking and experiences were mostly grounded in reality), yet were too disturbed to be labeled masochists, were classified as borderline.

Therapists used the word "fringe" to describe patients who had some difficult memories of recognizing both the good and bad qualities in people at the same time, who lived insecure and clamorous lifestyles, and who were often truly upset. Many of these opinions on BPD were based only on the impressions of a small number of patients and did not rely on rational research. Various exams have been conducted by professionals from those early days. These studies' findings have identified a number of critical traits that comprise what we now term borderline personality disorder, such as difficulties managing emotions, inappropriate behavior, and relationship and personality issues.

Individuals with BPD are never regarded to be on the edge of psychosis or anxiety again. Science is assisting us in keeping the views about BPD that seem to be correct and discarding the old thoughts about BPD that appear to be incorrect.

BORDERLINE PERSONALITY DISORDER SYMPTOMS AND FEATURES

BPD is a tumultuous state of insecurity and emotional disturbances. Individuals with BPD are uneasy about their emotions, reasoning, relationships, personality, and behavior. Individuals with BPD have strained relationships and are often afraid of being abandoned. Individuals with BPD experience their sensations as though they are on a thrilling roller coaster, with their emotions flitting from one extreme to the other.

They may also have difficulties with indignation (either experiencing outrage upheavals or being so scared of outrage that they avoid it entirely). Individuals with BPD behave rashly (they act quickly and without thought) when they are distressed, and they sometimes attempt suicide and engage in self-harm. Individuals with BPD often have problems making sense of their identity, and they may have difficulty thinking clearly and keeping grounded when they are frightened.

A persuasive BPD therapy goes as follows:

DYSREGULATION OF FEELINGS

This refers to insecure emotions (including rapid state of mind shifts) and difficulty managing sentiments. Individuals with BPD struggle with their emotions and are often overwhelmed by them.

In fact, some experts believe that emotional dysregulation is the most serious issue for those with BPD. In fact, some people believe that the bulk of the problems that people with BPD struggle with are caused by emotional dysregulation.

Temperamental thoughts and mindsets, as well as difficulty regulating resentment, are two signs of BPD that come under this category.

MOODS AND TEMPERAMENTAL EMOTIONS

Individuals with BPD often react to things that others are unlikely to respond to in the same way. For example, if you have BPD, you may be easily enraged by things that other people say or do, or you may discover that you become frightened more effectively than others. Only a basic or opposed glance may be enough to send you into an exciting spiral. Because people with BPD react honestly to such a wide range of stimuli, their emotions often ebb and flow like a roller coaster. They may be happy one minute and then depressed or irritable the next. Difficulty or Extreme Anger Anger Management

ANOTHER FEATURE OF BPD IS INTENSE ANGER OR DIFFICULTY CONTROLLING ANGER.

People with BPD may be successfully irritated or angered by things that do not irritate others.

They may also be unable to control themselves when they erupt, throwing objects, yelling at others, or feeling so consumed by wrath that they have no idea what to do

. Despite the fact that indignation is one marker of BPD, we have found that sentiments of shame, pity, and guilt are often more entrenched and difficult to adjust to in those with BPD. A few persons with BPD tend to use more energy being angry with themselves than with anybody else.

DYSREGULATION IN RELATIONSHIPS

The term "relational dysregulation" refers to difficulties in forming relationships with others. It does not mean that you are a bad or unlikeable person. Individuals with BPD are often intriguing, enticing, interesting, and delicate. By the way, they will generally combat their connections in two ways: temperamental ties and fear of relinquishment.

RELATIONSHIPS THAT ARE PRECARIOUS AND INTENSE

Individuals suffering from BPD often develop "rough" relationships that are raucous and insane. In fact, their sporadic bursts of desire make it difficult for them to maintain ties. If you have BPD, you may notice that things go exceptionally well in your relationships at times, and then everything seems to self-destruct at other times. You might be joyful, adoring, and happy one minute and then be indignant, disdainful, and depressed about your relationships the next.

The core idea is that relationships, like emotions, seem to be an exhilarating trip, bouncing back and forth between being amazing and utterly dreadful. If you have BPD, your relationships may also contain countless disagreements, conflicts, and even physical or psychological abuse.

DYSREGULATION OF THE CONDUCT

Conduct dysregulation denotes that your behavior is out of control (and perhaps harmful or dangerous) and has a negative impact on your life. Individuals with BPD often struggle with this condition in two ways: dangerous hurried behavior and self-harm.

DYSREGULATION OF SELF AND IDENTITY

When a person has self and personality dysregulation, he or she does not have a realistic or consistent sense of who they are and may feel emptiness for a substantial portion of the time.

DYSREGULATION OF THE SUBJECTIVE

When a person has subjective dysregulation, he or she experiences bad thinking as well as a disconnection from self or reality. It is important to note that these types of diseases are not common and occur more often when people with BPD are under a lot of stress or are really disturbed.

WHEN EXPERIENCING STRESS, SUSPICIOUS THOUGHTS, OR DISSOCIATION

One disorder is now skeptical, negative, or "distrustful" of others' motives. If you have this illness, it does not mean that you are stupid, psychotic, or mad. It suggests that when you are nervous, you become more suspicious or concerned about how others see you. You may come to assume that others are aiming to be cruel to you, exploit you, or misbehave with you on occasion.

You may also feel that others are looking at you and having unfavorable or critical thoughts about you (for example, "He's big," "She's repulsive," or "I don't care for her"). These interactions are more likely to occur when you are under stress or frustrated, but they are less likely to occur when things are going well. Separation is another aspect of psychological dysregulation. Separation is the sensation of being stared at, dispersed, in a cloudy mental state, unaware of your surroundings, or feeling as if you are not within your body.

Some people represent themselves as if they are floating to the ceiling and gazing down on their bodies and the people around them.

Separation occurs under pressure in the presence of BPD. Separation might be a good strategy to move away from difficulties. If your boss dismisses you and you are anxious, restless, and enraged, you may look at yourself intellectually for a little while to escape from your problems or sadness.

The problem with separating is that it doesn't solve anything, and you may do things while separating that are risky (for example, suicide attempts) or that you don't remember afterward (for example, unsafe single-night rendezvous).

HOW DO YOU DETERMINE IF YOU HAVE BPD?

As previously said, the best way to determine whether you have BPD is to consult with a professional who can do an analysis. Specialists and clinicians are two types of psychological well-being professionals who do research. Therapists are clinical professionals who have received specialized training in prescription-based and mental medications.

Both therapists and analysts are often in a good position to conduct a thorough assessment and reach a judgment. Others who contribute to discoveries include social workers, those with graduate degrees in brain science, and people with graduate degrees in leading brain science.

We recommend that you seek out a professional with training and experience in personality disorders and that you have a thorough assessment. Because BPD contains a long-standing example of identifying with the world (and is something that many people have struggled with throughout their lives), diagnosing BPD may take some time.

Regardless matter how tough it is to be patient when you actually need to figure out what's wrong with you, making a crucial decision is critical, and it may need a few preparations and a lot of discussions. It is also critical that the expert you deal with understands how to distinguish BPD from other conditions that may resemble BPD, for example, bipolar disorder or major depression.

Chapter 2

Symptoms Of Borderline Personality Disorder

People with BPD have broad mood fluctuations, as well as feelings of instability and insecurity. Borderline Personality Disorder has an impact on how you feel about yourself, how you interact with others, and how you are treated. Not everyone suffers from a borderline personality disorder.

Borderline Personality Disorder (BPD) patients may experience emotional fluctuations and ambiguity about how they see themselves and their position in the world.

Borderline personality disorder patients prefer to view things again and over, whether they are nice or terrible. People's perceptions of them might shift quickly.

An someone who is seen as a friend one day may be regarded as an opponent or a traitor the next.

These shifting emotions might result in passionate and unstable partnerships. Some individuals only have a few symptoms, while others have numerous. Symptoms might be induced by apparently innocuous circumstances. For example, sufferers with a borderline personality disorder may get furious and unhappy at the smallest separation from individuals they care about, such as while traveling on business.

How long they last depend on the intensity and frequency of their symptoms, as well as their age and the severity of their sickness. According to the Diagnostic and Statistical Manual Diagnostic Framework, some of the key signs and symptoms may include:

Friends and relatives go to great lengths to prevent giving up, whether genuine or imagined.

Unstable personal connections that oscillate between ideas such as "I'm in love!" "I detest it!"

- Chronic emotions of rage or emptiness
- Inappropriate, intense, or uncontrolled rage

- This is often followed by shame and remorse.

Irrational Sensations are disconnection from your own ideas or experiences of identity or "out of body" feelings of worry and tension associated with stress. Severe instances of stress might also result in brief psychological crises.

Taking drastic measures to prevent serious separation or rejection dread, whether real or imagined.

Rapid shifts in self-identity and self-image include shifting objectives and values, as well as making oneself feel horrible or as if you no longer exist.

Stress-related paranoia and brief intervals of touch with reality lasting from a few minutes to a few hours

We are safeguarding success through influencing and addressing dangerous behaviors like gambling, reckless driving, unsafe sex, drinking, binge eating, or drug use, or abandoning a good career, or terminating a nice relationship.

In reaction to the threats of suicide or the dread of being treated or wounded, people are often separated or rejected.

The extensive mode may endure from a few hours to a few days and might involve strong delight, irritation, shame, or worry.

Continual sensations of emptiness

Inappropriate, extreme rage, such as recurrent outbursts of rage, sarcasm or bitterness, or physical conflict.

Attempts to prevent giving up, whether actual or imagined, such as beginning a close (physical or emotional) connection or trying to cut off contact with someone

Impressive and frequently risky activities, such as financial problems, unprotected sex, drug misuse, reckless driving, and consuming foods. If this mode happens largely during a high mood or energy phase, it may be an indication of a flaw rather than a disruption of the status quo.

Suicidal ideation or threats

Severe and very changeable mode, with each occurrence ranging from a few hours to a few days.

Feelings of emptiness on a regular basis

Inappropriate, excessive rage, or trouble managing rage

It is difficult to trust, which is frequently accompanied by an unjustified dread of other people's motives.

Feelings of customization, such as being cut off from yourself, seeing oneself from outside one's body, or feeling unrealistic

Symptoms Have Been Explained

Because they are afraid that other people may desert them, as a result, they may leave individuals who can't leave other people - in settings where other people won't notice or take it personally.

Borderline Personality Problem is distinguished by an emotional disorder, which is an immediate, recurrent, and traumatic mood that is beyond the victim's control. Individuals with an issue find it challenging to build and sustain connections as a result of this condition.

They also struggle to regulate their own disorganized and sloppy conduct and often have opinions about who they are.

Borderline personality disorder patients often have a history of strong relationships that start and finish abruptly.

This is often caused by two factors:

Their dread of being abandoned

Their propensity to reprimand and then condemn others

However, when another student rejected to offer to be sociable for the first time, the young lady became afraid and hurt. He became suspicious that his new buddy was leaving him and attacked another student, beating him and accusing his friend of abandoning him.

Understandably, the other student discontinued the connection.

Such bouts are common and may be overpowering for persons suffering from a borderline personality disorder. Fear, discomfort, anxiety, wrath, grief, and shame might continue for a few hours or a few days.

Borderline personality disorder sufferers, on the other hand, pause when they are furious or overwhelmed. Some individuals commit suicide by severing their limbs and legs or by engaging in other types of self-harm.

People may participate in the following activities:

- Excessive drug and alcohol use
- They can't go shopping since they can't afford it.
- Gamble excessively
- Having bad eating habits
- Cleaning and Benching

In more aggravating conditions, the individual may attempt suicide or ponder about suicide in great detail. Most persons engaged in this condition are continually analyzing their own relationships for flaws and anticipate being abandoned by others. They desire to label themselves, people, and things as "all good" or "all evil," with no medium ground.

This is why little issues may often lead to the breakdown of a relationship. Regardless of how soon their relationship ends, many persons with borderline personality disorder are scared of being alone because they believe they are incapable of dealing with their difficulties on their own. Borderline personality disorder in warfare may be exhausting and upsetting.

People with this condition are in constant physical, emotional, and psychological discomfort. They have no idea who they are.

In one minute, the individual may consider himself to be a decent person, and in the next minute, he may consider himself to be terrible and impoverished. Thoughts regarding other individuals vary as well. That individual wants to trust others yet does not believe others are trustworthy. All of this perplexity might easily lead to the following emotions:

- Empty
- Sad
- Hollow

People suffering from borderline personality disorder may feel as if they leave their bodies in moments of stress and are unable to recall what occurred. These severe bouts of loneliness exacerbate their fragile sense of self. Similarly, and as unsettling, there is a period of deceit that may occur during times of stress or sadness.

I have extremely strong and unstable connections (for example, being someone else's ideal and then despising them terribly). Being unsure of oneself - not knowing who one is or what one should think of oneself. Maybe hazardous (e.g., money before spending money, risky sexual behavior, use of dangerous drugs or alcohol, reckless driving or eating bananas) or indecent (e.g., money before spending money, risky sexual behavior, use of dangerous drugs or alcohol, reckless driving or eating bananas).

Repeated self-harm, suicide, or suicidal ideation.

I am having brief yet acute emotional 'lows,' anger, or worry. This is normally just for a few hours at a time, although it may occasionally persist longer. To have the persistent sense of being 'empty' from inside.

They have very severe fury that is proportional to what causes it and being unable to resist it (for example, having a mood or waging a battle). Others may have acute uncertainties or strange experiences of being detached from their emotions, body, or environment while under stress.

The following are some symptoms of Borderline Personality Disorder that are explained:

Fear of giving up

- Unstable Relationships
- Blurring or altering your picture
- Poor Self-Treatment
- Self-Harming
- Extreme Emotional Swings
- Feelings of emptiness on a regular basis
- Explosive Temper
- Suspicious or out of touch with reality
- Fear of giving up

People with BPD often feel abandoned or lonely. Even something undesirable, such as a loved one getting home late or leaving on the weekend, is terrifying. This might be a desperate effort to keep the other person near.

You may plead, kiss, start arguing, follow your girlfriend's whereabouts, or physically prevent this individual from leaving.

Unfortunately, this conduct has the opposite effect on others, driving them away.

Unstable relationship

Relationships are harsh and short-lived for people with BPD.

You may quickly fall in love, assuming that every new person would make you feel better, only to be disappointed.

Your relationships seem to be either flawless or fantastic, with no in-between. Your loved ones, friends, or family members may feel emotionally drained as a consequence of your swinging from ideal to lack of appreciation, rage, and contempt.

Blurring or altering your picture

When you have BPD, your emotions are frequently unstable. Sometimes you like yourself, while other times, you despise or even despise yourself.

You may spend money you don't have, eat recklessly, drive recklessly, lift a store and indulge in unsafe sex, or misuse drugs or alcohol. These harmful activities may make you feel better in the moment, but they may harm you and the people around you.

Self-Harming

I was self-harming conduct that included suicide threats or attempts.

Suicidal and intentional self-harm are widespread in persons with BPD. Suicidal conduct includes contemplating suicide, giving suicidal suggestions or threats, or actually attempting suicide.

Self-harm refers to any effort to damage oneself without the desire to commit suicide. Biting and burning are two common methods of self-harm.

Extreme Emotional Swings

BPD is characterized by unstable emotions and moods. You might experience the exhilaration one minute and the frustration the next. Little things that other people brush over might throw you into an emotional tailspin.

These mood fluctuations are intense, but they pass quickly (unlike the emotional swings of depression or bipolar disease), lasting just a few minutes or hours.

Feelings of emptiness on a regular basis

People with BPD often describe feeling empty, as if there were a hole or a vacuum within them. Because you are restless, you might attempt to fill the emptiness with drugs, food, or sex. But nothing is really gratifying.

People with BPD often battle with skepticism or doubts about the intentions of others. When under duress, you may even lose contact with reality. You may feel fuzzy, disconnected, or as if you're out of your body.

Chapter 3

Using Mindfulness To Manage Emotions

Overcoming narcissistic abuse is one of the hardest things you could possibly go through. It takes a lot of work to find the impetus to move on from the agony that has enveloped your life to a brighter future. Pain is the most natural response to maltreatment. Your life has been wrecked, your heart has been crushed, and you have lost everything. However, everything is not lost. There are options for you, practical ones that can allow you to reclaim your life.

Meditation

Victims of narcissistic abuse suffer from emotional damage. The kind of trauma you suffer in such a relationship has long-term consequences for your life.

Meditation is one of the most powerful methods for healing, mitigating, and overcoming the negativity caused by a narcissist.

Meditation may help with almost any ailment that is caused or aggravated by stress. Meditation relaxes your body, lowering your metabolic rate, increasing your heart rate, and decreasing your blood pressure (Huntington, 2015). It also improves the operation of your brain waves and allows you to breathe more easily. As you learn to relax via meditation, the tension in your muscles pours out of your body from where the tension dwells.

The wonderful part about meditation is that it may be done even if you have a hectic schedule. You just need a few minutes every day to get started, and you'll be well on your road to recovery. Concentrate on your breathing during meditation. Pay attention to the movement of air in and out of your body. By tracking the route the air travels in and out of your body, this motion helps you concentrate. It is one of the simplest methods for calming down.

As the air travels in and out of your body, attempt to scan it to locate places of high tension. Observe your thoughts to become aware of what you are attempting to conquer via meditation. It's alright to feel overwhelmed, but don't pass judgment on yourself. Recovery isn't a race. It may take a few sessions, but your dedication will bring you through.

Do not dismiss your feelings. Your emotions are an important element of who you are. It is natural to respond in a certain manner to someone's actions or conduct toward you. Accept your emotions and conquer your negativity. Meditation can help you improve the health and strength of your neural connections to and from your brain by boosting the density of grey matter. You re-learn to be aware of your feelings and emotions, and over time, you sever the poisonous bond you had with your narcissistic abuser.

Trauma and distress disturb regions of the brain that control planning, memory, learning, attention, and emotional regulation. Meditation has proved to be an effective strategy in overcoming these issues by enhancing the function of the hippocampus, amygdala, and prefrontal cortex over time.

As a victim of narcissistic abuse, once your abuser has control of your life, you have no choice but to obey them.

Meditation, on the other hand, puts you back in charge of your life. You may recover your reality, heal, and gain the strength to conquer whatever problems you had while under their influence.

Therapeutic group therapy

When recuperating from narcissistic abuse, group therapy is one option to explore. One of the first things you'll discover in group therapy is that you can't heal your narcissistic abuser. What you will learn, though, is how to cope with narcissism.

Most of the time, victims are counseled to leave such violent relationships since they may only create pain and suffering.

In their desire for adoration, attention, and fulfillment, narcissists are merciless. They are aware that what they desire is impossible to attain, so they fool themselves into believing that they can force you to do it for them.

Group therapy for narcissistic abuse is beneficial because it provides you with something you haven't had in a long time: support. You know you are not alone when you hear about the experiences of other group members. The overpowering sensations you've been experiencing lighten when you realize there are others out there who can identify with what's been eating you inside.

While group therapy provides advantages, you must participate in order to reap these advantages.

The fact that you are taking the initial step to seek treatment demonstrates your determination to mend. Make a commitment to the treatment sessions by pledging what you want to gain from them. Participate after you've been accepted. It may be difficult at first since you must open yourself to strangers, but you will get the hang of it. At first, it is OK to sit and listen to people relate their stories. You can open up once you're at ease. Remember that as you continue to share, it will get easier. Never, ever hold back. Therapy is a secure environment. Sharing your story not only lets the group in on your anguish, but it may also help someone else in the group open up about theirs.

Cognitive-behavioral treatment (CBT)

Cognitive-behavioral therapy (CBT) is a therapeutic method that combines cognitive therapy and behavioral therapy to assist patients in overcoming traumatic situations that have robbed them of control. Cognitive therapy is concerned with the impact your ideas and beliefs have on your life, while behavioral therapy is concerned with recognizing and modifying undesirable behavioral habits (Triscari et al., 2015)

CBT is successful because your therapist does more than simply listen to you; they also serve as your coach.

It is a healthy exchange in which you discover important methods to assist you in better managing your life.

You become more aware of your emotional reactions, behavior, and perceptions.

CBT is appropriate for victims of narcissistic abuse because therapy teaches them how to comprehend their emotional experiences, recognize behavioral patterns, particularly harmful inclinations, and learn how to maintain control over some of their most challenging circumstances.

Cognitive-behavioral treatment

CBT is divided into CPT and CBT is divided into CPT and CPT is divided into CBT, and CPT is divided into It is one of the most often suggested approaches for treating trauma sufferers. Victims of narcissistic abuse often experience a great deal of trauma and may acquire PTSD. When you acquire PTSD, you may have a skewed perception of your surroundings, your life, and the people you contact with.

PTSD has an impact on your life view in the following ways:

- **Security**

After being abused, you are conditioned to be fearful of yourself and others around you. PTSD may amplify these safety concerns. You're frightened you won't be able to care for yourself or others.

- **Rely on**

Narcissists tear you down to your core. They make you feel as though you can't trust anybody or yourself. In the aftermath, PTSD might make you doubt your ability to make the proper decision.

- **Control**

You don't just lose control of your life; you rely on your abuser to lead you through it. This is what narcissism does to you.

Narcissists like having control over your life because it demonstrates that they have your attention and can do anything they want with you. After leaving a narcissist, PTSD may reinforce a sense of loss of control, making it difficult to get back on your feet.

One of the most terrible aspects of surviving a narcissist is how they destroy your confidence. Even some of the most self-assured persons in history have found themselves unable to understand who they are or what their lives are about. You avoid circumstances that need confidence and intelligent decision-making, which you would have gladly accepted in the past. Your self-perception is that you are a damaged, worthless person.

- **A close relationship**

Triangulation, among other deceptive techniques used by narcissists, makes you feel uncertain about yourself and closeness. You're uneasy because no one understands you, but you also don't understand why people treat you the way they do. Following narcissistic abuse, PTSD may cause flashbacks to times when your closeness was uneasy. It might be tough to form new connections as a result.

All of these ideas culminate in bad feelings that cloud your life, such as wrath, guilt, worry, despair, and fear. CPT teaches you valuable strategies for dealing with these emotions. Negative emotions instill a false sense of self in your subconscious, making you feel like a lesser entity. CPT may assist you by restoring your view of yourself and the world around you.

You learn how to confront the abuse and have a more positive and healthy outlook on life.

- **Yoga**

Yoga may provide a path to recovery for a trauma victim. Yoga's restorative advantages have long been used for wellbeing in Eastern traditional communities. Yoga assists you in establishing a link between your mind and your body. It keeps you grounded. This is one of the things you will need if you are to survive a narcissistic relationship.

Yoga has already been shown to be useful in healing a variety of physical and mental disorders, as well as trauma-related issues and stress (Criswell, Wheeler, & Partlow Lauttamus, 2014). Yoga, by combining breathing techniques, physical activity, and relaxation, helps you grow awareness and become more aware of your internal and external world.

Breaking up with and walking away from a narcissist is just the first step. Healing requires further stages. You'll need to get your bearings. You must put a stop to the chaos that has enveloped your life to the point that you no longer have an identity.

You will concentrate on breathing techniques during yoga. Breathing is one of the most efficient and inexpensive methods of obtaining relief. All you have to do to get through a tough time, emotional upheaval, or anxious moment is to breathe.

Find a comfy area to sit quietly and relax whenever you feel the need to bring the narcissist back into your life. Close your eyes and take a deep breath. Concentrate on your breathing, counting your breaths to distract yourself from the difficulty. Gentle yoga lessons might be beneficial in this regard.

- **Therapeutic art**

Art therapy is based on the belief that creativity may promote mental health and rehabilitation. Art is more than simply a talent; it is also a strategy that may be utilized to improve one's mental health. For many years, art therapy has been employed in psychotherapy. Patients may express themselves via art without having to speak to someone about their feelings.

It is perfect for persons who have difficulty expressing themselves vocally. Art can help you learn how to connect more effectively with others, handle stress, and even discover more about your personality. Experts think that via art therapy, their patients may learn how to solve difficulties, manage disputes, relieve stress, acquire good conduct, build or refine interpersonal skills, and raise their esteem and awareness (Lusebrink, n.d.)

Art therapists have a variety of methods at their disposal to assist you in overcoming the pain of a narcissistic relationship. There is so much to work with, from collages to sculpture and painting. People who have endured emotional trauma, despair, anxiety, domestic abuse, physical violence, and other psychological disorders as a result of an abusive relationship with a narcissist can consider art therapy.

The distinction between an art therapy session and an art class is that the focus in therapy is on your experiences. Your imagination, emotions, and ideas are important. These are the things a narcissistic spouse may have conditioned you to give up. Your therapist will urge you to express yourself from deep inside before you master some fantastic painting skills and methods. Instead of concentrating on what you can see with your eyes, you learn to create things from your imagination or feelings.

- **EMDR**

Another therapy for healing from narcissistic abuse is eye movement desensitization and reprocessing (EMDR).

It is a strategy that assists in reprogramming your brain away from trauma in order for it to learn how to reprocess memories. When you are exposed to repeated trauma, your brain may create a pattern that repeats the negative you have encountered for a long period (Mosquera & Knipe, 2015)

Victims experience a great deal of psychological pain as a result of traumatic recollections.

Because you don't have to go through your emotions and difficulties, EMDR is a one-of-a-kind therapeutic procedure. Instead, the brain is encouraged to shift the feelings you experience months or even years after you leave a narcissist.

EMDR works because eye movement allows the brain to open up, making it easier to access memories in a way that the brain can reprocess in a safe setting different than the one where your trauma was perpetuated. After accessing your memories, you may replace them with more empowered sensations and ideas, allowing you to detach from the pain and embrace more rewarding reactions to the triggers in your surroundings over time. Flashbacks, nightmares, and worry go away as you embrace a new life and break free from their grip.

Your brain recalls the traumatic experiences of verbal, sexual, psychological, emotional, and even physical abuse for victims of narcissistic abuse. During an EMDR session, you are advised to concentrate on the specifics of any such traumatic occurrences while seeing something else for a brief period of time.

What happens is that your memory changes as you focus on both the negative memories and a new positive affirmation. You will also learn self-soothing strategies to assist you in continuing to dissociate from the discomfort. EMDR assists in breaking free from life's chains and allowing your brain to think about events in new ways.

- **Self-hypnosis**

For many years, hypnotherapy has been used effectively to assist victims of narcissistic abuse in rehabilitating. However, certain circumstances must be satisfied in order for this to operate. You must be in the presence of particular stimuli that may induce hypnosis. You will also learn how to restrict your concentration and awareness, as well as how to allow yourself to freely experience your emotions without making a conscious decision to do so.

Narcissists are incapable of true connection; instead, they

reflect their victim's thoughts and worries about loneliness and abandonment. How does one enter a trance state for hypnosis? Emotional abuse has a large influence on your life.

You may easily relax using hypnosis. One of the last things you may have experienced during your ordeal with a narcissist is effortless relaxation. When you can allow yourself to relax without striving, you open the way to mending your mind and body.

- **Self-hypnosis**

It is a transforming process that pushes you to develop vital emotional techniques that may help you heal from abuse and protect yourself in the future. You get stronger and more peaceful with each session. The waves of emotional turbulence you used to feel subside, and you find yourself at peace with yourself and your surroundings.

Self-hypnosis also helps you have a better understanding of what your life is all about. You let go of the bad energy and embrace tranquility. You've been put on a road of rediscovery. You appreciate yourself more than you did throughout your narcissistic relationship. As the sessions progress, you will discover how to take the required steps toward healing and moving on in life. The most significant aspect of self-hypnosis is that you begin to look forward to a new life and genuinely believe in your potential to achieve while doing so.

- **Aromatherapy**

Even though you feel as if you are on the brink of a cliff with no way back, it is possible to recover from narcissistic abuse. Many individuals have done it before you, and you can too.

Recovery from this kind of trauma is really rewarding. Every time you make progress, you can look back and see how far you've come and how much you've changed. It teaches you to cherish your life and understand how poisonous it was before.

- **Aromatherapy**

It is one of the deliberate efforts you make to heal and recover from narcissistic abuse. Consider aromatherapy in the same manner that you would consider exercise. You work out on a regular basis if you believe you are out of shape. You may keep in shape by scheduling three or four training sessions every week.

The same is true for aromatherapy. Narcissists make you emotionally inadequate. You must train your emotions in order to live a happy and rewarding life. To alleviate emotional suffering, you must activate your amygdala. One of the most effective methods to trigger the amygdala is via smell. There is a significant link between your emotions and your sense of smell that has existed since you were a youngster.

The smell is directly linked to emotional relationships, whether favorable or bad. This explains why, whenever you smell your favorite dish being made, it reminds you of a moment when you had it. As a result, the smell may aid in evoking feelings of warmth and nostalgia. If odors can transport you back in time, they may also aid in reminding you of the painful events that occurred as a result of narcissistic abuse.

Chapter 4

Epidemiology, Factors Of Borderline Personality Disorder

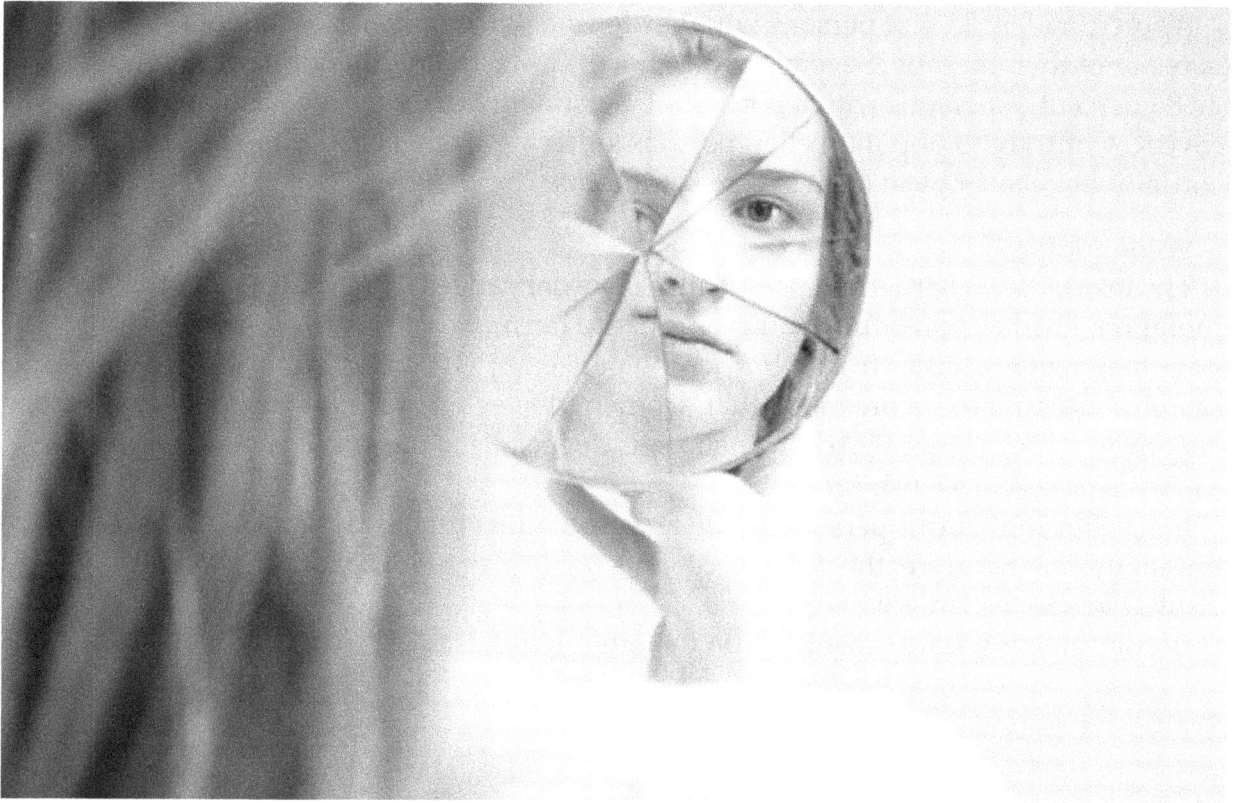

Hippocrates and Homer both accounted for the coexistence of intensely variable feelings such as impulsive anger, mania, and sadness that define borderline personality disorder.

The word was resurrected in the late 1600s by Swiss physician *Theophile Bonet,* who defined the occurrence of unstable emotions followed by unpredictability. However, Adolf Stern invented the word "borderline" in 1938 to characterize a group of patients who he felt had moderate schizophrenia and borderline psychosis and neurosis. The illness was termed as such because individuals displayed borderline signs of such disorders.

Approximately 35% of persons with borderline personality disorder obtain remission as a result of their therapy. Several studies have shown that with long-term therapy, more than 86 percent of persons with a borderline personality disorder may achieve sustained recovery. Contrary to popular belief, persons suffering from a borderline personality disorder may recover even from severe symptoms.

Epidemiology

The incidence of borderline personality disorder ranges from 1% to 2% of the overall population. Furthermore, due to an excess of the hormone estrogen, women are more prone than males to suffer from a borderline personality disorder. According to 2008 research, males are more prevalent than women to have a borderline personality disorder (5.6 percent vs. 6.2 percent). According to some specialists, the prevalence of borderline personality disorder is insignificant.

It is believed that this personality disorder accounts for at least 20% of all psychiatric admissions. Furthermore, this illness accounts for 10% of all outpatient psychiatric consultations in the United States.

Borderline personality disorder, on the other hand, is a

frequent ailment that has impacted convicts throughout the nation. Among the United States, the total prevalence of borderline personality disorder in the jail population is 17%. The high incidence of drug abuse and mood disorders in US prisons is connected to the high prevalence of convicts engaging in substance abuse and mood disorders.

People with borderline personality disorder, as previously stated, may recover from their illness. However, due to the patient's outpouring of emotions, the recovery might be harrowing. Even while this is true, persons with this illness may nevertheless live regular, healthy lives. The therapy and management options for those suffering from borderline personality disorder are listed below.

Psychotherapy

Psychotherapy is the most often used treatment for borderline personality disorder. Treatments are often depending on the patient's requirements. Patients suffering from borderline personality disorder should engage in long-term psychotherapy to improve their chances of managing their illness. There are several forms of psychotherapy therapies that patients may get, and the following is a description of the various types of psychotherapy treatments accessible to individuals suffering from this illness.

Treatment based on mentalization:

This is a kind of psychodynamic treatment. It is intended particularly for persons who have a borderline personality disorder. The goal of this therapy is to improve the patient's mental condition by enabling them to regain mentalization so that the psychotherapist can deal with the patient's present mental state. Individual or group treatment is often used for this surgery. This strategy seeks to help the patient to form attachments to their peers.

Psychotherapy based on transference:

This sort of psychotherapy is carried out twice a week. It is quite regimented and was designed exclusively for people with a borderline personality disorder. The goal of this therapeutic practice is to lessen patients' self-harming behavior.

Dialectical behavior therapy (DBT):

This kind of psychotherapy tries to lower the risk of self-harm, suicidal conduct, and drug misuse in people with mental illnesses.

General psychiatric management:

This psychotherapy treatment technique is an evidence-based approach to treating mental diseases. Cognitive-behavioral therapy and psychoanalytic object relations therapy are two treatments utilized in general psychiatric management.

Schema-centered therapy:

Schema therapy is an integrated approach to treating a broad range of mental and personality disorders, including borderline personality disorder. It treats patients by combining methods and ideas such as cognitive behavioral therapy, attachment therapy, and psychoanalytic object relations theory.

The success of psychotherapy treatment choices is heavily dependent on the individuals. However, research shows that both mentalization-based treatment and dialectical behavior therapy are successful in treating all subtypes of BPD.

However, the difficulty with psychotherapy is that it is a long-term treatment that may place significant financial pressure on the patient and his or her immediate family. A long-term psychotherapy session for individuals with a borderline personality disorder is quite costly, but many researchers are currently producing shorter versions of the treatment alternatives in order to make the treatment available to as many people as possible.

However, the expense of psychotherapy is not the only factor that makes this treatment option difficult to pursue. Because patients with this disease are afraid of rejection, psychotherapists must be adaptable while dealing with the patient's negative attributions.

Meditation Studies show that meditation may help people with borderline personality disorder make positive changes in their brains.

Meditation may also help to alleviate the symptoms associated with a borderline personality disorder. Indeed, many psychiatrists advocate meditation as an additional treatment to psychotherapy.

Admissions to Outpatient and Inpatient Facilities

The majority of people with borderline personality disorder have a higher chance of recovery if they get outpatient or inpatient treatment. There are several institutions around the nation that provide full-time treatment to patients suffering from various types of mental diseases, including borderline personality disorder. The difficulty with this sort of management approach is that it is highly costly. Thus only a few people can afford to get treatment from these institutions.

So, which therapy option should a person with borderline personality disorder choose? There is no definitive solution, and it is critical to urge a borderline person to consult a psychiatrist who will build an appropriate treatment plan to manage the patient's condition.

Treatment Moderating Factors for Borderline Personality Disorder

There are moderating variables that may alter the success of treatment choices for people suffering from a borderline personality disorder, just as there are for other forms of personality disorders. This section will go through the many elements that affect the success of therapies as well as the recovery of people suffering from this ailment.

Executive Power

The executive function relates to a person's cerebral skills. It is how we respond to various stimuli that are put at us. Borderline personality disorder patients' executive processes moderate the link between their symptoms and their susceptibility to rejection. This suggests that the symptoms have a significant impact on the brain's cognitive functions. For example, a person with borderline personality disorder's brain mandates that he or she behave more on impulse, which reduces the effectiveness of therapy that a patient receives.

Family Situation

The immediate familial environment also influences the development and rehabilitation of a borderline personality disorder patient.

Self-Complexity

A patient with borderline personality disorder exhibits several features and feels a broad range of emotions at the same time. This self-complexity makes treating persons with borderline disorder very challenging for psychiatrists. The problem is that individuals with this illness go through such an internal conflict full of ironies that it is difficult to assist them to grasp that they should only have a linear channel for their emotions.

Thought Suppression

Thought suppression is a typical defensive technique in those suffering from a borderline personality disorder, and it is the deliberate endeavor to avoid considering specific ideas that may make them vulnerable. Patients with borderline personality disorder become more secretive and resistant to therapy as a result of thought suppression.

A borderline personality disorder is one of the most easily identified personality disorders, but it is also one of the most difficult to treat since individuals are aware of their illness yet are resistant to change. Nonetheless, with consistent treatment and patience, it is still feasible to assist them in recovering.

Chapter 5

Diagnosis Of The Disorder

One of the most difficult aspects of dealing with this kind of disease is determining its cause. Most individuals who have it will refuse to interact with the doctor or psychiatrist who is attempting to help them. Therefore they will ignore them and refuse assistance. Often, it is the responsibility of family members to identify the problem and undertake the necessary treatment before the person with the disease receives it. They will not go in on their own since they will not recognize that they have any problems.

Once you've gotten the individual with the condition through the door, the diagnosis will be based on the examination performed in the clinic by a mental health specialist. The easiest method to accomplish this is to provide the patient with the many characteristics of the illness, which are described above, and ask them whether any of these criteria describe them. This will engage the person in the remedy, increasing the likelihood that it will succeed.

Furthermore, a doctor is unlikely to have enough time or outside experience with the patient to evaluate if the qualities exist on their own, and this may give them a typically accurate way of doing so.

When you enable the individual with the disease to actively participate in the diagnosis, they will be more eager to receive the aid that the expert will provide. Some physicians, however, think that it is preferable not to disclose to their patients that they have this diagnosis because they believe it is fraught with stigma and that the individual may be resistant to treatment since they may have heard in the past that this is an incurable condition. While this is one option, there is a lot of research that shows that the person suffering from the condition should be aware of it in order to get the most effective therapy possible.

During this examination, the patient will be asked several questions regarding their symptoms, such as when they started and how severe they were. They may also be asked questions about how these symptoms are affecting their lives. Some of the difficulties that the doctor will take specific notice of include any ideas about hurting others, any experiences with self-harm and any suicidal thoughts that the individual has.

The diagnosis will be based on what the patient has said throughout sessions, as well as what the doctor has been able to see in their brief time together. These two factors will generally be able to combine to provide a positive view of what is going on. There are a few more tests that may be used to establish whether a person has a borderline personality disorder. Some laboratory tests or a physical exam may be performed to help rule out some of the other factors that might provoke similar symptoms, such as the individual misusing narcotics or having thyroid disease, both of which can produce some of the same behaviors as a borderline personality disorder.

Once a patient's problem has been identified and diagnosed, it is time to get to work on getting them the therapy they need to be healthy and reclaim their life. While this will be a lot of effort and will take some time, it is necessary if the individual wants to reclaim their lives and be happier.

Here's some additional information on how the disease may be identified and how the individual can obtain the care they need to feel well quickly.

Classifications Internationals

You will be able to locate a few categories that are utilized globally to aid with diagnosis. These categories are useful because they enable the physician to make a diagnosis without relying on their own personal ideas, and they keep everything orderly and consistent throughout.

The World Health Organization recognizes the concept of borderline personality disorder.

Type I is impulsive.

The first kind of category identified in this is the impulsive type. At least three of the factors listed below must be present in order to diagnose someone with this kind of disease.

A strong propensity to lose control or to act out.

This will occur suddenly and will not be the result of someone instigating the problem or pushing them to act out. Often, the act will be performed by the individual without them fearing or even thinking about the implications of their actions. This is merely something they're going to do, maybe over a little dispute or other problem that shouldn't have been such a big deal but was made into one.

A notable tendency is for the sufferer to engage in quarrelsome conduct, and they will have many disagreements with others around them. This will be particularly true for impulsive activities that have been condemned or prevented. This is a person who habitually picks fights with others around them and sees every slight as an opportunity to get into a large brawl.

When it comes to violence or rage, this person is prone to violent outbursts. They not only have these problems, but they also lack the capacity to regulate the explosions or other complications that arise. They will seem to be exceedingly furious, but they will also appear to lack the ability to cool down even if they wanted to.

These folks will also struggle to stick to their plan if they do not get a reward straight soon.

They may have been really engaged in completing it, but when it did not bring the instant benefit that they desired, they grew disappointed and furious and chose to abandon it.

This would happen rather often, and the individual would only persevere with activities they knew they could complete and be rewarded for.

These folks often have erratic and unpredictable emotions that alter practically without notice. It may be difficult to keep up with this kind of individual.

These are the five criteria that are often present in people suffering from the impulsive form of this condition. You will observe that they will often perform things without thinking about what they are doing or what will happen after they are through, which may be harmful. To be diagnosed with this kind of condition, a person must have at least three of the above-mentioned factors present while speaking with their therapist in the office.

Borderline Type

The next category is the borderline type. This one will be a little bit different. This will take a bit from the list above and then combine it with a bit from the list shown below. To be diagnosed with this category, you must have at least three of the impulsive type's symptoms present, as well as at least two of the ones listed below. Among the things to watch for are:

This personality type often experiences confusion and disruptions in their self-image, as well as internal preferences and life goals. They do not believe they are valuable, and although they seek engagement with others, they are unsure why these individuals would want to interact with them. They may wonder about a lot, bewildered, since they don't know who they are, what they should do with their life, or what will happen to them.

They may also be more likely to get engaged in relationships that are often volatile and stressful. This might include those whirlwind romances where they meet and marry in a few months, but it does not have to be this extreme.

Because the connection is so unstable, it will not endure, and because it was so passionate, it is likely to produce an emotional crisis in the individual suffering from the condition.

These individuals will go to great lengths to ensure that they are never abandoned. They are afraid that one day they may wake up with no one to be their friends or to assist them when they are in need. This is worsened further by the fact that they push others away and are not particularly skilled at seeing other people's points of view. They will labor almost compulsively to ensure that people do not leave them alone so that they may always have the assistance and company that they need.

They will also face regular threats and acts of self-harm.

This is often not done in an effort to persuade someone to behave in a certain manner or to influence someone else's sentiments. This is rather something they do in the hopes of calming their own feelings. They will struggle greatly with their own emotions, and if they are unable to manage them, they may resort to self-harm in the hope of finding comfort.

Emptiness is a frequent emotion that surrounds them. They will feel hollow since they have no plans for their future or for the things they desire to accomplish in their life. They don't have any long-term objectives or plans, so they'll typically simply roam about and hope that everything works out. This may lead to a fairly empty existence.

They will often display impulsive conduct. This will include problems like drug misuse and speeding.

The concept behind performing these activities is that it offers the sufferer a break from the negative sensations or uncontrollable emotions that they are experiencing, allowing them to feel better for a short period of time. The problem arises when the individual starts to feel a little guilty about their actions, causing them to feel much worse than they did before. As previously stated, a number of factors must be present before someone may be diagnosed with this version of the condition. Those who fit these criteria, however, should get assistance as quickly as possible.

Members of the family

Even the manner in which the individual with the condition treats others around them might be used to diagnose them. People with this illness are significantly more likely to dislike their family members, and they are often upset at these same people. Often, the person with the illness may seek to isolate themselves from the family because they are upset by a little slight or are concerned that family members will notice a problem. Often, family members may feel powerless and furious about how they are connecting to this individual and may question what they can do to make things right again.

Research conducted in 2003 discovered that after family members learned that the behavior was for a cause, their attitudes would shift. In most situations, as the individual with the disorder's family members realized what was going on, their anger and hurt against them increased. While this may not seem to be the case, it is often thought that these sentiments arise as a result of the family being given incorrect information about the disease, causing them to blame the individual rather than the problem at hand.

The greatest method for family members to aid someone they care about is to learn as much as they can about the disease. It is tempting to start browsing through books and viewing programs on the disease, and although this may be a fine place to start in certain circumstances, you will frequently discover that the material is incorrect. Get out there and discover the correct facts, and this will help you make more sense of what you are witnessing with your loved one.

This will be just as tough for family members to deal with as it will be for the individual experiencing the problem. They are the ones who have been emotionally hurt by their loved one's refusal to interact with them. It is critical that the family get the treatment and assistance that they need to feel better about their circumstance. Understanding the whole scenario and how it affects the family and the sufferer might make it simpler to work through it all together.

Other Disorders Diagnosis

It is very unusual for someone living with this kind of condition to also have additional problems, whether they be other personality disorders or something else, to manifest at the same time. This makes detecting the personality disorder even more difficult since it may be concealed by some of the other symptoms present. When compared to people who have other personality disorders, persons with borderline personality disorder are more likely to satisfy the criteria for additional disorders such as:

Mood illnesses, such as bipolar disorder and significant depression, will be included.

Anxiety disorders — many of them may be treated, including post-traumatic stress disorder, social anxiety disorder, and panic disorder.

Personality disorders of other types

Abuse of substances

- Bulimia and anorexia nervosa are examples of eating disorders.
- Attention deficit hyperactivity disorder (ADHD)
- Somatoform disorders
- Disorders of dissociation

If a person has this personality disorder and one of these other difficulties, they should not be labeled with the personality disorder until that other issue is resolved. These other disorders might cause some of the same symptoms as the personality disorder, and treating them can be an easier way of dealing with them.

This is unless the signs of the personality disorder can be shown to have existed for many years prior to the other condition.

Furthermore, women are more prone to encounter some of the concerns described above, whilst males are more likely to experience others.

Men, for example, will have a larger prevalence of drug use disorders, whilst women will have a higher prevalence of eating disorders. If you want to see some of the finest outcomes with treating your borderline personality disorder, it is critical that you address these additional problems. If you have any of the other concerns stated above, it will be almost hard to treat the personality disorder since they will exacerbate the disease and will keep it continuing even if you go through a lot of treatment.

This is why most specialists would conduct a thorough check of the patient to see whether there are any other concerns present. Once the other concerns are resolved, it may be much simpler to treat the personality disorder. For the greatest outcomes, this may be accomplished with some preparatory treatment or with the use of drugs to manage concerns such as anxiety and depression.

Chapter 6

Treatment and Medication

Each individual's experience with a borderline personality disorder is unique. Some symptoms may be more prominent than others; for example, one may be more paranoid, while another may be more dissociative.

A therapist may propose the best therapy for borderline personality disorder based on the condition and circumstances.

When someone has BPD, it may be a frightening experience that leaves them feeling alone since it strains connections. Individuals with BPD need the assistance of therapists to overcome this element of the condition and return to their regular lives, where they may benefit from the pleasure that good human interactions can provide.

Treatment for BPD may teach individuals essential skills that they can use in the real world to sustain interpersonal connections. Furthermore, therapy may alleviate the stress associated with prescribing medication that reduces BPD symptoms.

Psychotherapy

Psychotherapy is the most often used treatment for persons suffering from mental diseases, particularly those suffering from BPD. Although there are many different types of psychotherapy, they all have one purpose in common: to help patients better understand how their ideas and emotions work. It is an essential element of treatment because, although medicine may help lower some symptoms of BPD, it does not teach patients how to gain coping skills or control emotions in the same way that psychotherapy does.

Psychotherapy is also important in preventing individuals from committing suicide. This is why therapists and other medical experts are engaged to keep in contact with the patient during the therapy, continually assessing their risk of suicide. When a patient develops suicidal thoughts, hospitalization is the next step.

Dialectical Behavioral Therapy (DBT)

Dialectical Behavior Therapy, or DBT, is the most well-known and successful kind of psychotherapy today. Marsha Linehan established it, and it is a program that teaches individuals how to better handle their lives and emotions. DBT also emphasizes emotion control, self-awareness, and cognitive restructuring. DBT takes a comprehensive approach and is generally done in a group setting. However, since the skill set taught by Dialectical Behavior Therapy is deemed sophisticated, it is not suggested for persons who have trouble learning new ideas.

Validation and dialectics are two ideas used in dialectical behavior therapy. The client is taught to acknowledge that their feelings are genuine, appropriate, and legitimate during validation. Dialectics, on the other hand, is a kind of philosophy that teaches that life is not black and white. It also emphasizes the significance of embracing ideas even if they contradict one's own convictions.

DBT therapists help suicidal people to improve their mindfulness, interpersonal effectiveness, emotion control, and distress tolerance. When persons with BPD realize that there are healthy methods to cope and handle one's emotions, the likelihood of self-harm and suicide decreases considerably.

Borderline personality disorder, like other types of personality disorders, is difficult to cure. Treatment is frequently protracted since the objective is to transform a person's perspective about the world, stress, and other people. BPD treatment normally lasts at least a year, although it may last much longer.

Other types of psychotherapy that are used to treat borderline personality disorder include conflict resolution and social learning theory. These are more solution-focused treatments that fail to address the primary problem that persons with BPD face, which is trouble regulating their emotions.

Schema-Focused Therapy

Schema Focused Therapy is a style of psychotherapy that focuses on identifying and treating harmful patterns of thinking. Schema-focused treatment incorporates aspects from cognitive-behavioral therapy (CBT) and integrates them with other types of psychotherapy.

Schema-focused treatment is based on the idea that if a person's core developmental needs, such as love, acceptance, and a need for safety, are not met, it leads to the formation of maladaptive ways of thinking about the world.

These are known as maladaptive early schemas. Schemes are broad patterns of behavior and thought. They are more than just beliefs since they are deeply ingrained patterns that influence how one views and interacts with the environment.

According to the schema theory, schemas emerge when occurrences in one's current life have a similarity to events in one's history that are directly connected to the construction of the schema. When a person develops unhealthy schemas as a consequence of a tough upbringing, they will adopt bad ways of thinking as a reaction to the circumstance. Furthermore, schema theory says that the symptoms of BPD are frequently produced by a rough childhood in which a child may have suffered abandonment, trauma, or mistreatment by one or both parents, leading to the formation of maladaptive early schemas.

Schema-focused treatment for borderline personality disorder aims to uncover significant schemas in a person's life and connect them to schemas existing in previous occurrences. A therapist works with the patient to help them process the emotional responses that develop as a result of the schema. They then strive to address maladaptive coping mechanisms in order to help the patient react to the scheme in a healthy way.

Exercises aimed to stop destructive behavioral patterns, improve the way one thinks, and encourage the patient to release their anger may be included in schema-focused therapy.

Transference Focused Therapy (TFT)

Transference Focused Therapy makes use of the patient-therapist interaction to help a person with borderline personality disorder perceive the world more clearly. Transference is defined as the process through which emotions are passed from one person to the next. It is a crucial notion in psychodynamic treatments in which it is proposed that the way a client feels about people who are essential in their life be transferred to his therapist. Transference therapy allows the therapist to fully grasp how the patient interacts with the people in his life in order to help them learn to manage relationships properly. Ultimately, the purpose of transference-oriented treatment is to assist patients in re-enjoying solid relationships.

Transference-focused therapists think that symptoms of borderline personality disorder that come from dysfunctional interactions experienced as a kid persist into adulthood, impairing these people's capacity to maintain normal, healthy relationships.

The interactions we experience with our main caregivers as children influence how we build a sense of ourselves and how we see other people. If a kid does not have a healthy connection with their caretakers, they will have trouble connecting to others and having a positive self-image as adults.

Evidence suggests that childhood abuse, trauma, or loss of caregivers increases one's chance of developing a borderline personality disorder. And, since these symptoms have a negative influence, preventing individuals from building connections later in life, some BPD specialists think that it is critical to address this by assisting people in focusing on better relationships via transference-focused treatment.

The interaction between the patient and the therapist is the center of this kind of treatment. Unlike other types of therapy in which the therapist instructs the patient on what to do, transference-focused therapy entails the therapist asking the client multiple questions throughout the session as they explore responses.

Furthermore, there is a greater focus on events that occur in the current moment rather than searching for prior experiences. For example, rather than addressing concerns with caregivers from one's past, the conversation focuses on how the client interacts with their present therapist.

Transference-based therapists are also good at staying impartial, which contributes to the effectiveness of this kind of treatment. They are aware that they are not to provide an opinion on their patient's response and that they will not be accessible outside of session hours unless in an emergency.

Therapy Based on Mentalization

Another kind of psychotherapy is mentalization-based treatment (MBT). MBT is predicated on the assumption that persons with borderline personality disorder have trouble thinking about their own ideas. This implies that persons with BPD are unable to assess whether their own ideas, beliefs, and views are realistic and valuable to them. Individuals with BPD, for example, may experience spontaneous inclinations to injure themselves and end up succumbing without considering the ramifications of their behavior.

MBT is also beneficial since it teaches individuals that others have their own ideas and beliefs and that your perception of their mental states is not always true. It also helps individuals recognize that their activities have an influence on the thinking of others.

The primary purpose of MBT is to assist clients in recognizing their own and others' mental states.

It also educates those suffering from BPD. how to take a step back from their own views and first determine whether they are valid

MBT may be performed as inpatient treatment in a hospital. Treatment consists of regular therapist appointments as well as group sessions.

MBT normally lasts around 18 months; however, depending on the patient's needs, some patients may be required to stay in the hospital for the whole period of their therapy. During the course of their treatment, certain hospitals and treatment centers will enable patients to depart at specific periods.

Therapeutic Neighborhoods

Therapeutic Communities (TC) are a kind of treatment in which individuals with a variety of psychological disorders engage in an organized setting. This kind of therapy is most suited for persons who struggle with emotions and are suicidal. Others with borderline personality disorder may manage their difficulties better if they are taught the skills required for good social engagement with a diverse spectrum of people. TC treatment is often residential, with individuals staying in households 1-4 days per week.

In addition to individual and group sessions, TC asks patients to engage in various activities aimed to develop social skills and building confidence. Doing home duties, preparing and cooking meals, playing games, and participating in leisure activities are examples of these activities. All participants in therapeutic communities are also required to attend regular community meetings where persons with various psychological problems gather to address issues and concerns within the community.

One of the therapeutic community method's distinguishing traits is that it is democratically governed. All members, including staff, are welcome to provide their thoughts on how TCs should be managed. They may even vote on whether a person should or should not be welcomed to the group. This implies that even if one's therapist believes that a therapeutic community is the best type of therapy for a case of borderline personality disorder, they will not be automatically admitted. Each TC defines acceptable conduct guidelines because they impose limits such as the ban of alcohol use and aggression against oneself and other members of the community. Members who violate the standards may be requested to resign from the TC.

Although a therapeutic community is one of the most extensively used therapy options for persons with borderline personality disorder, there is insufficient data to say if it is beneficial for everyone.

This is especially true for those with BPD who have difficulties adhering to regulations since TCs may be fairly severe with requirements.

Self-Care

During therapy, patients are frequently given a phone number to contact if they believe they are experiencing a serious crisis. It might happen when persons with BPD are having bouts of intense symptoms and are more likely to self-harm or commit suicide. A variety of people may be referred to community mental health practitioners, social workers, or other medical experts.

A crisis resolution team service, which specializes in caring for persons with major mental health concerns, may also be offered in your region. These teams often come to the aid of those who have attempted suicide and need to be hospitalized.

Those suffering from borderline personality disorder often discover that just talking to someone about their situation will help them get out of their crisis.

Certain circumstances, however uncommon, may need the use of medications such as tranquilizers to help one's mood.

Medications like this are often recommended for seven days in order to regulate emotions.

Individuals suffering from borderline personality disorder are urged to join support groups in order to get social support from others who are going through similar experiences. Assistance groups may provide moral support by sharing shared ideas and experiences. Patients may also practice coping techniques and learn how to manage their emotions with the help of new friends they meet at these support groups. They have been shown to be an important element in assisting persons with BPD to broaden their skillset while developing good social ties, thus reducing their symptoms in the long term.

If you suffer from a borderline personality disorder, you may find it difficult to take better care of yourself. Those who have been diagnosed with BPD, on the other hand, should make it a point to take better care of themselves since symptoms might worsen if self-care is neglected.

The fundamentals of self-care are participating in activities that promote relaxation and well health.

This includes getting adequate exercise, getting enough sleep, taking your therapist's recommended medicines, eating nutritious foods, and coping with stress in healthy ways.

Self-care is essential for everyone since people who take care of themselves are less likely to suffer from mental diseases. It is particularly crucial for persons suffering from BPD since it might not only increase symptoms but also result in delayed recovery.

When it comes to adequate self-care, many individuals overlook the value of regular sleep.

Medication

Some physicians think that medication may help persons with borderline personality disorder, while others disagree.

There is currently no authorized medicine for the treatment of BPD. However, several types of medication have been shown to be effective in lowering symptoms in select persons.

SSRIs (selective serotonin reuptake inhibitors) are often the first kind of medicine administered to patients. SSRIs are medications that are intended to lessen impulsivity, sadness, anger, suicidal behavior, and anxiety in patients who have mental health issues.

Medications such as antidepressants and anti-anxiety medications may be beneficial in reducing symptoms, particularly during a crisis or emergency.

Prozac, Zoloft, Nardil, Wellbutrin, and Effexor are the most often recommended antidepressants for people with a borderline personality disorder. However, since depression and anxiety are generally short-term symptoms that come and go as a consequence of numerous stresses in a person's life, this kind of drug is not recommended for long-term usage.

Antipsychotics have a good impact on patients even if they do not have BPD. In patients with borderline personality disorder, these are beneficial at lowering paranoia, anxiety, aggression, rage, and impulsivity. Haldol, Clozaril, Risperdal, Seroquel, and Zyprexa are examples of common antipsychotic drugs.

Another kind of drug used to treat symptoms of borderline personality disorder is mood stabilizers. These are beneficial in treating impulsive behavior, mood swings, and the profound emotional upheavals induced by BPD. Lithobid, Depakote, Tegretol, and Lamictal are examples of common mood stabilizers.

Anxiolytics are medications that specialize in lowering anxiety and are also recommended for BPD. While anxiolytics are prescribed to individuals with borderline personality disorder, there is inadequate data to support their efficacy in treating BPD as a whole. In fact, particular kinds of anxiolytics such as benzodiazepines have been proven to exacerbate the symptoms of BPD in other persons. Anxiolytics often used for BPD patients include Valium, Xanax, Ativan, Klonopin, and Buspar.

Before obtaining drugs from a doctor, it is critical to properly address possible negative effects. Other kinds of treatment may be investigated if the adverse effects seem to be detrimental, particularly if the negative effects appear to be higher than the benefits. Medication for a borderline personality disorder may differ based on the kind of medication utilized.

Some of the most prevalent adverse effects are listed below:

- Antidepressants:
- Headache
- Insomnia
- Appetite suppression
- Sedation

- Sexual impotence
- Putting on weight
- Acne Tremors are mood stabilizers.
- Putting on weight
- Discomfort in the stomach
- Antipsychotics: \Akathisia
- Mouth dryness
- Putting on weight
- Sexual impotence
- Sedation
- Anti-anxiety: Fatigue
- Sleepiness
- Mental sluggishness
- Memory issues
- Coordination issues

How to Determine Whether a Medication Is Effective

When you begin taking medication for borderline personality disorder, you may notice emotional and physical changes. If a medicine is effective, the first thing you may notice is a favorable shift in how you react to events. People feel the advantages of drugs in a different time period than others, despite the fact that the shift is generally gradual and modest. In fact, beneficial improvements are seldom realized until they have been occurring for some time. It is also normal for others to notice changes in your emotional reaction before you do, so ask folks you frequently hang out with whether they see any changes.

Chapter 7

Practicing Mindfulness

Each individual's experience with a borderline personality disorder is unique. Some symptoms may be more prominent than others; for example, one may be more paranoid, while another may be more dissociative.

A therapist may propose the best therapy for borderline personality disorder based on the condition and circumstances.

When someone has BPD, it may be a frightening experience that leaves them feeling alone since it strains connections. Individuals with BPD need the assistance of therapists to overcome this element of the condition and return to their regular lives, where they may benefit from the pleasure that good human interactions can provide.

Treatment for BPD may teach individuals essential skills that they can use in the real world to sustain interpersonal connections. Furthermore, therapy may alleviate the stress associated with prescribing medication that reduces BPD symptoms.

Psychotherapy

Psychotherapy is the most often used treatment for persons suffering from mental diseases, particularly those suffering from BPD. Although there are many different types of psychotherapy, they all have one purpose in common: to help patients better understand how their ideas and emotions work. It is an essential element of treatment because, although medicine may help lower some symptoms of BPD, it does not teach patients how to gain coping skills or control emotions in the same way that psychotherapy does.

Psychotherapy is also important in preventing individuals from committing suicide. This is why therapists and other medical experts are engaged to keep in contact with the patient during the therapy, continually assessing their risk of suicide. When a patient develops suicidal thoughts, hospitalization is the next step.

Dialectical Behavioral Therapy (DBT)

Dialectical Behavior Therapy, or DBT, is the most well-known and successful kind of psychotherapy today. Marsha Linehan established it, and it is a program that teaches individuals how to better handle their lives and emotions. DBT also emphasizes emotion control, self-awareness, and cognitive restructuring. DBT takes a comprehensive approach and is generally done in a group setting. However, since the skill set taught by Dialectical Behavior Therapy is deemed sophisticated, it is not suggested for persons who have trouble learning new ideas.

Validation and dialectics are two ideas used in dialectical behavior therapy. The client is taught to acknowledge that their feelings are genuine, appropriate, and legitimate during validation. Dialectics, on the other hand, is a kind of philosophy that teaches that life is not black and white. It also emphasizes the significance of embracing ideas even if they contradict one's own convictions.

DBT therapists help suicidal people to improve their mindfulness, interpersonal effectiveness, emotion control, and distress tolerance. When persons with BPD realize that there are healthy methods to cope and handle one's emotions, the likelihood of self-harm and suicide decreases considerably.

Borderline personality disorder, like other types of personality disorders, is difficult to cure. Treatment is frequently protracted since the objective is to transform a person's perspective about the world, stress, and other people. BPD treatment normally lasts at least a year, although it may last much longer.

Other types of psychotherapy that are used to treat borderline personality disorder include conflict resolution and social learning theory. These are more solution-focused treatments that fail to address the primary problem that persons with BPD face, which is trouble regulating their emotions.

Schema-Focused Therapy

Schema Focused Therapy is a style of psychotherapy that focuses on identifying and treating harmful patterns of thinking. Schema-focused treatment incorporates aspects from cognitive-behavioral therapy (CBT) and integrates them with other types of psychotherapy.

Schema-focused treatment is based on the idea that if a person's core developmental needs, such as love, acceptance, and a need for safety, are not met, it leads to the formation of maladaptive ways of thinking about the world. These are known as maladaptive early schemas.

Schemes are broad patterns of behavior and thought. They are more than just beliefs since they are deeply ingrained patterns that influence how one views and interacts with the environment.

According to the schema theory, schemas emerge when occurrences in one's current life have a similarity to events in one's history that are directly connected to the construction of the schema. When a person develops unhealthy schemas as a consequence of a tough upbringing, they will adopt bad ways of thinking as a reaction to the circumstance. Furthermore, schema theory says that the symptoms of BPD are frequently produced by a rough childhood in which a child may have suffered abandonment, trauma, or mistreatment by one or both parents, leading to the formation of maladaptive early schemas.

Schema-focused treatment for borderline personality disorder aims to uncover significant schemas in a person's life and connect them to schemas existing in previous occurrences. A therapist works with the patient to help them process the emotional responses that develop as a result of the schema. They then strive to address maladaptive coping mechanisms in order to help the patient react to the scheme in a healthy way.

Exercises aimed to stop destructive behavioral patterns, improve the way one thinks, and encourage the patient to release their anger may be included in schema-focused therapy.

Transference Focused Therapy (TFT)

Transference Focused Therapy makes use of the patient-therapist interaction to help a person with borderline personality disorder perceive the world more clearly. Transference is defined as the process through which emotions are passed from one person to the next. It is a crucial notion in psychodynamic treatments in which it is proposed that the way a client feels about people who are essential in their life be transferred to his therapist. Transference therapy allows the therapist to fully grasp how the patient interacts with the people in his life in order to help them learn to manage relationships properly. Ultimately, the purpose of transference-oriented treatment is to assist patients in re-enjoying solid relationships.

Transference-focused therapists think that symptoms of borderline personality disorder that come from dysfunctional interactions experienced as a kid persist into adulthood, impairing these people's capacity to maintain normal, healthy relationships.

The interactions we experience with our main caregivers as children influence how we build a sense of ourselves and how we see other people. If a kid does not have a healthy connection with their caretakers, they will have trouble connecting to others and having a positive self-image as adults.

Evidence suggests that childhood abuse, trauma, or loss of caregivers increases one's chance of developing a borderline personality disorder. And, since these symptoms have a negative influence, preventing individuals from building connections later in life, some BPD specialists think that it is critical to address this by assisting people in focusing on better relationships via transference-focused treatment.

The interaction between the patient and the therapist is the center of this kind of treatment. Unlike other types of therapy in which the therapist instructs the patient on what to do, transference-focused therapy entails the therapist asking the client multiple questions throughout the session as they explore responses.

Furthermore, there is a greater focus on events that occur in the current moment rather than searching for prior experiences. For example, rather than addressing concerns with caregivers from one's past, the conversation focuses on how the client interacts with their present therapist.

Transference-based therapists are also good at staying impartial, which contributes to the effectiveness of this kind of treatment. They are aware that they are not to provide an opinion on their patient's response and that they will not be accessible outside of session hours unless in an emergency.

Therapy Based on Mentalization

Another kind of psychotherapy is mentalization-based treatment (MBT). MBT is predicated on the assumption that persons with borderline personality disorder have trouble thinking about their own ideas. This implies that persons with BPD are unable to assess whether their own ideas, beliefs, and views are realistic and valuable to them. Individuals with BPD, for example, may experience spontaneous inclinations to injure themselves and end up succumbing without considering the ramifications of their behavior.

MBT is also beneficial since it teaches individuals that others have their own ideas and beliefs and that your perception of their mental states is not always true. It also helps individuals recognize that their activities have an influence on the thinking of others.

The primary purpose of MBT is to assist clients in recognizing their own and others' mental states.

It also educates those suffering from BPD. how to take a step back from their own views and first determine whether they are valid

MBT may be performed as inpatient treatment in a hospital. Treatment consists of regular therapist appointments as well as group sessions.

MBT normally lasts around 18 months; however, depending on the patient's needs, some patients may be required to stay in the hospital for the whole period of their therapy. During the course of their treatment, certain hospitals and treatment centers will enable patients to depart at specific periods.

Therapeutic Neighborhoods

Therapeutic Communities (TC) are a kind of treatment in which individuals with a variety of psychological disorders engage in an organized setting. This kind of therapy is most suited for persons who struggle with emotions and are suicidal. Others with borderline personality disorder may manage their difficulties better if they are taught the skills required for good social engagement with a diverse spectrum of people. TC treatment is often residential, with individuals staying in households 1-4 days per week.

In addition to individual and group sessions, TC asks patients to engage in various activities aimed to develop social skills and building confidence. Doing home duties, preparing and cooking meals, playing games, and participating in leisure activities are examples of these activities. All participants in therapeutic communities are also required to attend regular community meetings where persons with various psychological problems gather to address issues and concerns within the community.

One of the therapeutic community method's distinguishing traits is that it is democratically governed. All members, including staff, are welcome to provide their thoughts on how TCs should be managed. They may even vote on whether a person should or should not be welcomed to the group. This implies that even if one's therapist believes that a therapeutic community is the best type of therapy for a case of borderline personality disorder, they will not be automatically admitted. Each TC defines acceptable conduct guidelines because they impose limits such as the ban of alcohol use and aggression against oneself and other members of the community. Members who violate the standards may be requested to resign from the TC.

Although a therapeutic community is one of the most

extensively used therapy options for persons with borderline personality disorder, there is insufficient data to say if it is beneficial for everyone.

This is especially true for those with BPD who have difficulties adhering to regulations since TCs may be fairly severe with requirements.

Self-Care

During therapy, patients are frequently given a phone number to contact if they believe they are experiencing a serious crisis. It might happen when persons with BPD are having bouts of intense symptoms and are more likely to self-harm or commit suicide. A variety of people may be referred to community mental health practitioners, social workers, or other medical experts.

A crisis resolution team service, which specializes in caring for persons with major mental health concerns, may also be offered in your region. These teams often come to the aid of those who have attempted suicide and need to be hospitalized.

Those suffering from borderline personality disorder often discover that just talking to someone about their situation will help them get out of their crisis.

Certain circumstances, however uncommon, may need the use of medications such as tranquilizers to help one's mood.

Medications like this are often recommended for seven days in order to regulate emotions.

Individuals suffering from borderline personality disorder are urged to join support groups in order to get social support from others who are going through similar experiences. Assistance groups may provide moral support by sharing shared ideas and experiences. Patients may also practice coping techniques and learn how to manage their emotions with the help of new friends they meet at these support groups. They have been shown to be an important element in assisting persons with BPD to broaden their skillset while developing good social ties, thus reducing their symptoms in the long term.

If you suffer from a borderline personality disorder, you may find it difficult to take better care of yourself. Those who have been diagnosed with BPD, on the other hand, should make it a point to take better care of themselves since symptoms might worsen if self-care is neglected.

The fundamentals of self-care are participating in activities that promote relaxation and well health.

This includes getting adequate exercise, getting enough sleep, taking your therapist's recommended medicines, eating nutritious foods, and coping with stress in healthy ways.

Self-care is essential for everyone since people who take care of themselves are less likely to suffer from mental diseases. It is particularly crucial for persons suffering from BPD since it might not only increase symptoms but also result in delayed recovery.

When it comes to adequate self-care, many individuals overlook the value of regular sleep.

Medication

Some physicians think that medication may help persons with borderline personality disorder, while others disagree.

There is currently no authorized medicine for the treatment of BPD. However, several types of medication have been shown to be effective in lowering symptoms in select persons.

SSRIs (selective serotonin reuptake inhibitors) are often the first kind of medicine administered to patients. SSRIs are medications that are intended to lessen impulsivity, sadness, anger, suicidal behavior, and anxiety in patients who have mental health issues.

Medications such as antidepressants and anti-anxiety medications may be beneficial in reducing symptoms, particularly during a crisis or emergency.

Prozac, Zoloft, Nardil, Wellbutrin, and Effexor are the most often recommended antidepressants for people with a borderline personality disorder. However, since depression and anxiety are generally short-term symptoms that come and go as a consequence of numerous stresses in a person's life, this kind of drug is not recommended for long-term usage.

Antipsychotics have a good impact on patients even if they do not have BPD. In patients with borderline personality disorder, these are beneficial at lowering paranoia, anxiety, aggression, rage, and impulsivity. Haldol, Clozaril, Risperdal, Seroquel, and Zyprexa are examples of common antipsychotic drugs.

Another kind of drug used to treat symptoms of borderline personality disorder is mood stabilizers. These are beneficial in treating impulsive behavior, mood swings, and the profound emotional upheavals induced by BPD. Lithobid, Depakote, Tegretol, and Lamictal are examples of common mood stabilizers.

Anxiolytics are medications that specialize in lowering anxiety and are also recommended for BPD.

While anxiolytics are prescribed to individuals with borderline personality disorder, there is inadequate data to support their efficacy in treating BPD as a whole. In fact, particular kinds of anxiolytics such as benzodiazepines have been proven to exacerbate the symptoms of BPD in other persons. Anxiolytics often used for BPD patients include Valium, Xanax, Ativan, Klonopin, and Buspar.

Before obtaining drugs from a doctor, it is critical to properly address possible negative effects. Other kinds of treatment may be investigated if the adverse effects seem to be detrimental, particularly if the negative effects appear to be higher than the benefits. Medication for a borderline personality disorder may differ based on the kind of medication utilized.

Some of the most prevalent adverse effects are listed below:

- Antidepressants:
- Headache
- Insomnia
- Appetite suppression
- Sedation
- Sexual impotence

- Putting on weight
- Acne Tremors are mood stabilizers.
- Putting on weight
- Discomfort in the stomach
- Antipsychotics: Akathisia
- Mouth dryness
- Putting on weight
- Sexual impotence
- Sedation
- Anti-anxiety: Fatigue
- Sleepiness
- Mental sluggishness
- Memory issues
- Coordination issues

How to Determine Whether a Medication Is Effective

When you begin taking medication for borderline personality disorder, you may notice emotional and physical changes. If a medicine is effective, the first thing you may notice is a favorable shift in how you react to events. People feel the advantages of drugs in a different time period than others, despite the fact that the shift is generally gradual and modest.

In fact, beneficial improvements are seldom realized until they have been occurring for some time. It is also normal for others to notice changes in your emotional reaction before you do, so ask folks you frequently hang out with whether they see any changes.

Chapter 8

Building a Coping Skills Toolkit.

We all have our good days and terrible days. If you have BPD, experiencing either may be significantly more acute. It is useful to have a set of coping skills to assist you in swiftly identify solutions to cope with adversity. (or many) days as they come up. Consider this to be your coping skills.

Toolkit. Most of the time, this does not have to be a physical toolset. The contents will be conceptual in any case, however you may create a list of "things" to store in this pack and take around with you when you're feeling down, when you're overcome with emotion, and it might be tough to recall what you're supposed to be doing.

What your coping mechanisms are, or to think clearly about anything by , You can rapidly locate a solution if you have your list near at hand . With your feelings

The following is a list of the many sorts of tasks you can do.

Grounding abilities.:

These, like the ones mentioned before, may simply assist. You must concentrate on current physical and mental sensations. Make use of visuals or auditory stimuli to divert your attention away from the immediate unpleasant emotion. Pay attention to the noises around you, not just the apparent ones. All of the noises you can hear take note of how they behave.

Rise and fall

So you'll hear the thunder of cars on a busy street. Snatches of conversation, birdsong (maybe), or the noises of nature construction activity in the neighborhood Lose yourself in just about anything as long as it's safe.

For a little period, listen to the noises around you. Keeping a journal this is a technique that many people with BPD find beneficial. For identifying triggers, assessing emotions, and making lists of there are advantages and disadvantages. Be emotive in your writing; say whatever comes to mind. Desire to, as well as all you feel. Sometimes just expressing yourself is sufficient. You may get rid of bad ideas in this manner without putting yourself in danger. Others are being alienated! Never be concerned with little matters such as spelling. Grammar, or simply making sense, may be a challenge. Rant as much as you want on paper like!

Positive deeds consider effective exercises to help you get rid of your bad feelings. Emotions. Cleaning the house/oven, or just sitting and doing nothing knitting! Indeed, everything that is repetitious and necessitates. Concentration is a fantastic method to regulate your emotions and to improve your performance. Reduce the intensity of your encounters with them.

These are merely the most fundamental concepts for your Coping Skills Toolkit. They may be beneficial to many individuals, but you may also need to discover your own strategies for coping with the ups and downs of BPD. The crucial Make a list of them, keep it with you, and make as large a list as you can. You certainly can. Look for things that you can perform while you're in a safe place.

Ones that you can do at home (knitting, for example)

and ones that you can do wherever while you're out and about or at work (for example, basic mindfulness example). Have a solid mix of these so that no matter what the scenario is, you are prepared. You may choose a basic coping strategy that is appropriate for the circumstance. After you've made your list, practice; not all of the talents will come naturally. You may need to persist with some before they come easily to you do. By practicing, you are also strengthening positive mental abilities. And they'll be there for you when you need them. You'll discover this over time.

Knowing one of your normal reactions to stressful circumstances is to employ rather to on the previous, self-destructive path. As stated at the beginning of the book, this is the moment at which your BPD will become less of a concern on a daily basis, and you will be well on your way to recovery.

- The path to recovery
- Self-Esteem and BPD

Low self-esteem is a feature of the majority of BPD patients.

In many cases, BPD develops throughout adolescence and is the cause of adolescent suicide.

As a consequence of abuse or neglect this is typically due to emotional neglect. And the outcome of being taught that your opinions or feelings do not matter valid. People who have poor self-esteem often believe.

There isn't much to contribute to others or the world in general. There are many techniques to boost or restore your self-esteem, and in this part. We'll look at some fundamental techniques. While they are fundamental, you should keep them in mind. Consider employing all of them on a regular basis. Gradually establishing a feeling of Self-esteem is a difficult and time-consuming process.

These Exercises and assignments are short enough to be completed quickly and on a regular basis. And without being too difficult or burdensome. As you progress, Each time (often and frequently), you'll discover yourself creating a sound.

Basis for emotions of self-worth, as well as that you are addressing larger undertakings or activities that expand on this. Self-talk that is constructive. "I'm" is how you explain yourself to yourself. "Such a moron"? "I'm a waste of space," you say? "I'm not worth knowing," you say? We all feel this way from time to time, however these sentiments do not contribute to your success.

Self-esteem. When things go awry, it's customary to employ this kind of language. "Self-talk," especially for people with BPD. It is all about positive self-talk. Repositioning these emotions You forgot about an essential meeting? "I made a mistake; these things happen!" may be a more appropriate statement to do for yourself "Oh well, it's hardly the end of the world," one would say.

Another nice one - and it's accurate. Nobody living (or dead) has done it thus far. Committed a mistake that led in that result, and odds are, It will not be your fault if it occurs. Be a little gentler on yourself. Take command. You don't have to take charge of major issues to make a difference. Difference in one's life Organize a file system, or remodel a drawer a space Do something that will enable you to plan and then execute a plan.

A basic job Take it one step at a time so that your accomplishments pile up one after the other. The opposite you may think of greater ventures (such as bungee jumping or skydiving other personal obstacles) when your confidence grows – but only on a modest scale

Steps are a good place to start.

Perform some charitable or volunteer activities. This is quite advantageous since. It's all about contributing to society and feeling useful. This may be beneficial. It will help you to build a feelin that you have some value in the world, and it will help you to develop a sense that you have some worth in the world. It also gets you out and about with other folks. This, in and of itself, may be difficult, but establishing new acquaintances and broadening one's horizons. Expanding your horizons may provide a significant boost to your self-esteem.

Finally, attend your treatment appointments. Everything in this book is original. Geared at providing you with simple, fundamental concepts to assist you through. With BPD, you have to take each day as it comes. However, professional counselling is available. Sessions will be where you make the most progress, and they will. It not only enable you to develop yourself if you come on a regular basis regard, demonstrate your ability to regulate the situation, but also assist you in your final recovery

Final Thoughts

BPD is a common disorder, but it is the most frequent of all mental or emotional difficulties is the one with the greatest long-term and sustainable prospects recuperation. It may take years to completely recover, but it is critical to plan ahead of time. That objective from the outset If you have BDP or have just been diagnosed with it, It's also crucial to understand that emotions are a part of being diagnosed. Not in and of themselves terrible. They play a crucial role in our lives. Our psychological make-up is important in our everyday life.

Learning how to Accepting them, regulating them, and coping with intense emotions may be difficult. It is difficult, but it is not an impossible challenge!

Chapter 9

How To Improve Social Relationships

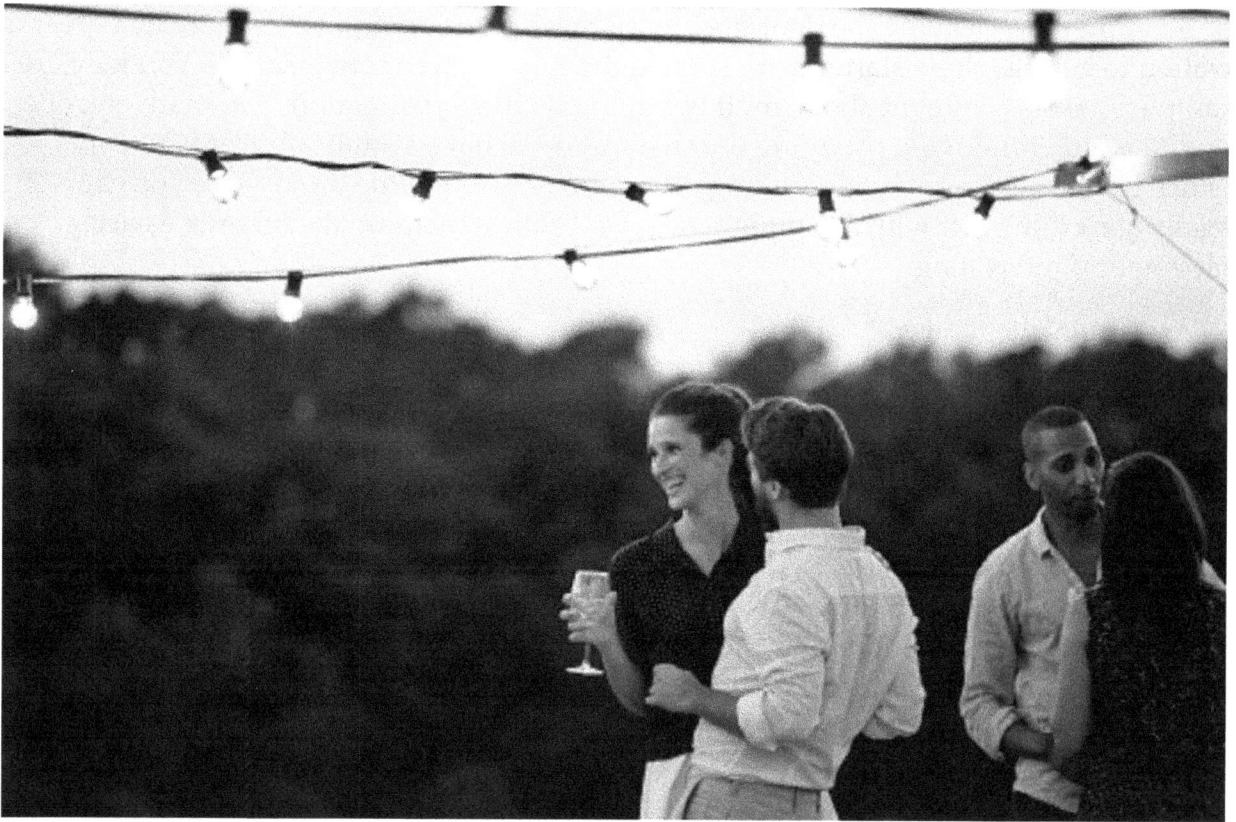

There aren't many guidelines that will help you leave a lasting impression. Follow the five steps outlined below, and you'll have the opportunity to meet and interact with a diverse variety of people in a social organization.

Turn on the light.

Many people may bombard the other person with "speak with style" queries when they first meet or get acquainted with them (Where do you live? What are you going to do? How do you want your action to go? And so on.) This kind of talk is not only taxing, but it's also quite unpleasant to react to a barrage of questions from someone about whom you have no knowledge.

So, rather than leaving the door open with these kinds of inquiries, you're in a great position to get this show started with some light, non-content conversation. You may, for example, make a comment about anything going on in your situation. Alternatively, open up with a little fun-loving prodding (but make sure to have a smile all over when you disturb her, so she knows you're joking). If you're not feeling the discussion, you can usually start things off with a compliment - maybe on something the other is wearing that you find interesting.

Assemble allegiance

It is vital to building affinity in any kind of social relationship, regardless of whether it is a commercial deal or meeting a young girl at a bar. How would you go about doing this? You may begin by adopting the "I" perspective when discussing your thoughts, feelings, and conclusions. For example, instead of proclaiming "b-ball is the greatest game ever," as if it's some goal certainty, say "I love b-ball," and possibly go into some detail about why you enjoy it.

This may seem to be a minor distinction, but using the "I" point of view allows others to see into your inner world - your thoughts, feelings, and so on. Furthermore, when you offer them this more meaningful glance, it encourages them to think of you as someone who has similar sentiments to them.

This creates a passionate association, causing others to sense a stronger relationship with you.

Make a contribution.

There is a special attitude that can greatly benefit you in social interaction. It might be difficult to obtain at times, but if you want to, people will want to associate with you as often as possible. That is the perspective of a supplier.

Don't expect to "receive" anything from your relationships. Don't contact a young girl only to gain her phone number or connect with a business VIP to ensure he'll show indicators of improvement work. If you want to build a good relationship with that young girl so she'll want to date you, or that VIP so he'll want to connect you with a job, start by delivering value first.

I want to have a good time with the young woman and brighten her day. Offer to help the VIP overcome any problem he is facing. Many people will feel pressured to give back if you keep your focus on consistently giving with no desire for obtaining anything in return.

That young woman will need to give you her phone number, and that VIP will need to help you acquire a fantastic job. This will not be the case all of the time, but in the long run, focusing on what you can offer rather than what you can gain can provide enormous rewards.

Make yourself helpless.

Individuals are concerned about how they will be run over in almost every kind of social collaboration. It's really energizing when someone comes along and tells them it's okay to remove that "social curtain." That they may stop fretting about trying to "appear cool" and fit in, and that they can be themselves and yet be recognized.

To lead the group and make oneself defenseless is an excellent technique to open this door and demonstrate to others that it's acceptable to relax, open up, and really behave naturally. For example, if you're unsure about anything (your weight, how you're dressed, how worried you are...), don't try to hide it and expect no one to notice. Rather, shine a bright light on it. Bring it up, and even mock yourself for it (but don't appear naturally dismissive).

Calling attention to your own imperfections and giggling at them can make other people feel better about their perceived flaws. As an added bonus, this is a fantastic way to forge really deep bonds.

Maintain an optimistic attitude

There is no social cooperation that can be improved with a negative mindset. The more productive and upbeat you can be in your collaborations, the more others will like working with you. All things considered, dispositions are contagious.

Furthermore, if you insist on being nice and productive in social cooperation, it will rub off on the people you're with. Furthermore, people will value your presence.

Improving Your Social Skills Through Powerful Communication

Building strong relationships with others may dramatically reduce stress and anxiety in your life. In reality, boosting your social help is linked to overall greater mental health since having fantastic companions may act as a "support" for feelings of discomfort and negative mood. However, for other people, their anxiety might contribute to their avoidance of social situations and prevent them from making relationships. This is especially true if you are socially anxious and really need to make friends but are either too terrified to even contemplate it or are unsure how to connect with people.

Regrettably, one of the consequences of keeping a deliberate distance from social situations is that you never get the opportunity to:

Improve your self-assurance through connecting with others.

Develop strong relationship skills to increase the possibility of making productive connections.

For example, if you are afraid of going to gatherings or asking someone out on the town, your lack of experience and low assurance will make it even more difficult to know how to cope with these situations (such as what to dress, what to say, and so on). Frequently, people have the necessary abilities but lack the confidence to put them to use. In any case, practice will increase your confidence and enhance your interpersonal skills.

What Is the Importance of Communication Skills?

Relational qualities are the key to forming (and maintaining) friendships and forming a strong, socially supportive group of individuals. They also help you cope with your own wants while also being aware of the needs of others. Individuals aren't born with outstanding interpersonal skills; they are discovered via exploration and repeated practice, just like any other talent.

Three areas of communication that you may need to practice are:

- Nonverbal communication
- Emphasis on discussion abilities

Note: clearly, there are several perspectives to engaging correspondence, and you may want more explicit help in some areas (for example, finding out how to handle conflict, introductory abilities, offering criticism, and so on.). If it's not too much bother, look at the "Prescribed Readings" list at the end of this module for more specific guidance.

Communication Through Nonverbal Means

Nonverbal communication accounts for a large portion of what we communicate to one another.

What you say to others with your eyes or nonverbal communication is just as powerful as what you say with words.

When you are nervous, you may behave in ways that are meant to keep you from conversing with people. For example, you may avoid direct eye contact or speak softly. At the end of the day, you're doing whatever it takes not to transmit in order to avoid being assessed negatively by others. In any event, your nonverbal communication and speaking style send powerful signals to people about you: ecstatic state (for example, eagerness, dread)

Attitude toward the audience (for example, accommodation, disdain) information on the subject

Sincerity (do you have a secret plan?)

As a result, if you keep a strategic distance from eye contact, keep a safe distance from people, and speak quietly, you are likely conveying, "Avoid me!" or "Don't interact with me!" Most likely, this isn't the message you need to deliver.

Discussion Abilities

Starting and maintaining conversations is perhaps the most difficult challenge for someone who suffers from social anxiety. It isn't uncommon to clash with a piece while seeking to create informal conversation since it isn't always straightforward to consider remarks. This is especially noticeable when you are restless. On the other hand, some agitated people continue on and on, which might have a bad effect on others.

Self-assuredness

Self-assured communication is the sincere expression of one's own needs, wants, and feelings while considering those of the other person. When you communicate forcefully, your approach is non-compromising and non-critical, and you accept responsibility for your own actions.

If you are socially anxious, you may have difficulty conveying your thoughts and feelings in a clear manner. Self-assurance talents may be difficult to adopt, especially when being self-assured might involve keeping oneself away from the way you would normally get things done.

For example, if you are afraid of conflict, you may continually obey the group and refrain from expressing your opinions. As a result, you may have developed a distanced communication style. On the other side, you may expect to dominate and govern people, and you may have developed a strong communication style.

Regardless, an expressive communications style has significant benefits. For example, it may help you relate to people more authentically, with less uneasiness and hostility. It also provides you with greater control over your life and reduces feelings of impotence. Furthermore, it grants OTHER people the right to live their lives.

Chapter 10

How To End Anxiety

Whatever position you play in life, the ability to correctly regulate and express your emotions will undoubtedly be important. You must also be able to recognize, interpret, and react correctly to the emotions of others around you. Consider how you would feel if you couldn't detect when one of your close friends was upset or when one of your colleagues was furious at you. Emotional intelligence is defined as the ability to not only express and manage one's own emotions but also to read and comprehend the emotions of others.

To put it simply, emotional intelligence refers to your capacity to notice, manage, and analyze emotions, whether they are your own or those of others. Some individuals have a high level of emotional intelligence and can regulate their emotions in a variety of settings while also reacting to the emotions of others around them. On the other hand, some people have little emotional intelligence; these are the people who would burst at nearly anything and scarcely regard the sentiments of others.

Let's look at the differences between those who have emotional intelligence and those who don't. Our first character is someone who accepts life as it comes. They recognize that most of the time, when things go wrong, it is beyond their control, rather than perceiving it as the world personally targeting them. They seldom become offended, particularly over trivial matters, and they understand when to express their feelings.

Furthermore, this individual is sensitive to how others are experiencing.

They do not reply in kind when a colleague walks in and begins shouting at them. They see that something must be upsetting that individual and take action to assist or solve the issue at the core of the situation. When one of their buddies is having a difficult day, they speak it out and try to make that person feel better.

Let's take a look at our second individual now. This individual has a difficult time managing their emotions.

When they are unhappy about anything, they may lash out at others (whether it is their fault or not), weep easily, and may experience anxiousness. These people often believe that the world is against them and those little events, which do not mean all that much, will set them off.

This is scarcely a notion when it comes to reacting to others. They will disregard their friends' concerns and just interpret events depending on how they directly affect them. When someone else is upset with them, they believe they are being treated unjustly. The world is against them, and no one understands them.

Our first encounter was with someone who had a high degree of emotional intelligence. This individual is able to detect and manage their emotions, as well as pick up on the emotions of others around them. The second individual lacks emotional intelligence. They become furious over everything, have no concept of why they feel the way they do and don't even consider the sentiments of others. Of course, there are differences between these two extremes, and determining your own degree of emotional intelligence may be useful in assisting you to grow.

Some individuals feel that by putting forth the effort, you may develop your emotional intelligence.

Others, however, feel that this is an inborn trait, something that you are born with that is exceedingly difficult, if not impossible, to alter. Both schools of thinking are probably correct in some ways.

We are all born with an inherent amount of emotional intelligence that we may either cultivate and increase or let fallow due to misuse.

Emotional intelligence is divided into four components.

Your emotional intelligence will be determined by four major criteria. These are some examples:

Perceiving emotions:

The first step toward understanding emotions is to learn how to sense them correctly.

This includes learning to understand nonverbal cues such as facial expressions and body language.

Reasoning with emotions:

The next step is to utilize your emotions as a means of promoting cognitive activity. This may be difficult at first, but emotions can help us prioritize what we are paying attention to and responding to, and we can use this to learn more about ourselves.

Understanding emotions:

The feelings that we experience might have a variety of meanings. For example, if you see someone is upset, you may need to take a step back and consider why they are feeling that way. A boss may be angry at you for your job because they got in trouble with their employer, battled with their wife, received a speeding ticket, or a variety of other reasons, and someone with strong emotional intelligence will be able to understand this.

Managing emotions:

the skill to successfully regulate your emotions comes next. As part of your emotional management, you must be able to control your emotions, discover a suitable reaction, and then respond.

Your emotional intelligence may be measured in a variety of ways. There are various tests that can be used to verify this, but you can also find out your own emotional intelligence and modify it via hard work and dedication. You may simply develop your emotional intelligence by learning how to understand your feelings, what is producing them, and the proper reaction to the circumstance at hand.

So, why would you want to devote your time to developing emotional intelligence?

A high degree of emotional intelligence may make a significant impact in a variety of circumstances in your life. In the office, for example. Employees with a greater degree of emotional intelligence perform better because they choose employment that they are enthusiastic about, work well with others, convince others to their views, and avoid disputes. Consider how some of these talents may benefit you in your own job, whether you're looking to develop or just remain on top. Everyone might benefit from brushing up on these abilities in order to perform better at work.

Another critical area where you will experience the benefits of working with emotional intelligence is in your relationships, whether with a spouse, family, or coworkers. Each individual you meet will have their own set of emotions, and being able to understand them and react appropriately will make it much simpler for you to get along with them. When disagreement does develop, you will be able to keep your emotions in control, averting a larger explosion than is required regardless of the kind of relationship you are attempting to repair.

Everyone can develop their emotional intelligence, and there are several advantages to doing so. It is crucial to note, however, that it is a talent that takes time to acquire.

You will not be able to wake up after a few days of practice and have complete control over your emotions. In fact, you will most likely have to concentrate on this for quite some time before it becomes a habit.

However, if you grasp this from the beginning and work hard to monitor, comprehend, and regulate your emotions, you will be able to achieve your objectives in no time.

The most common challenges encountered while employing the EMDR technique

- Q.: I don't have time to show an awful image while also moving my eyes.

   A.: You do not need to think about the image when moving your eyes. You concentrate on it at first, and then you may entirely concentrate on the motions themselves, returning to the image after they are completed.

1. Q.: I picked one image to study, but after the first round of motions, another one emerged in front of my eyes, which was similarly unpleasant but related to a totally different issue.Should I keep working on the existing image or start a new one?

A.: In such instances, it is best to trust your internal process. If a new image emerges spontaneously, it is worthwhile to work with it.

Exercise it till it no longer causes pain. After that, return to the original aim with which you began working.

- Q.: I don't recall everything about the scenario. I merely have a hazy or partial remembrance.

    A.: Absolute precision is not essential. Take in the stuff that is now accessible to you. With the use of EMDR, even incomplete memories may be efficiently sorted out. In some cases, after 2-3 rounds of EMDR, the image begins to take on more distinct contours, and new features that you did not recall previously may begin to surface in it. However, this is not required.

    When you can't recall the scenario entirely, focus on the sentiments it evokes in you.

- Q.: The image stayed intact after two rounds of EMDR, and the intensity of negative feelings only intensified.

    A.: This is a true possibility: the process of working through bad information involves a momentary increase of an unpleasant sensation.

This is normal and occurs when a personattempts to separate himself from an uncomfortable experience. When using the EMDR approach (like with EFT), it is critical not to reject the unpleasant feelings linked with the pictures that you are working with.

- Q.: The feelings are really too intense. When I attempt to solve the problem, I experience such overwhelming emotions that I am unable to continue. I'm scared I'll become much worse in this situation.

  A.: In such a case, apply the emotional freedom method (EFT) to calm your nerves and stabilize your condition. Perhaps you still have insufficient resources to deal with this painful situation. In this instance, I put off working on this episode for a while.

While you are working on less tough memories, utilize EFT to learn how to better manage your present state - all of this will help you to enhance your stress resistance resource.

After a time, you'll be able to return to working on the most difficult memories. Another option is to get professional assistance from an expert with experience coping with serious emotional damage.

Chapter 11

What Does It Mean To Rewire Your Brain?

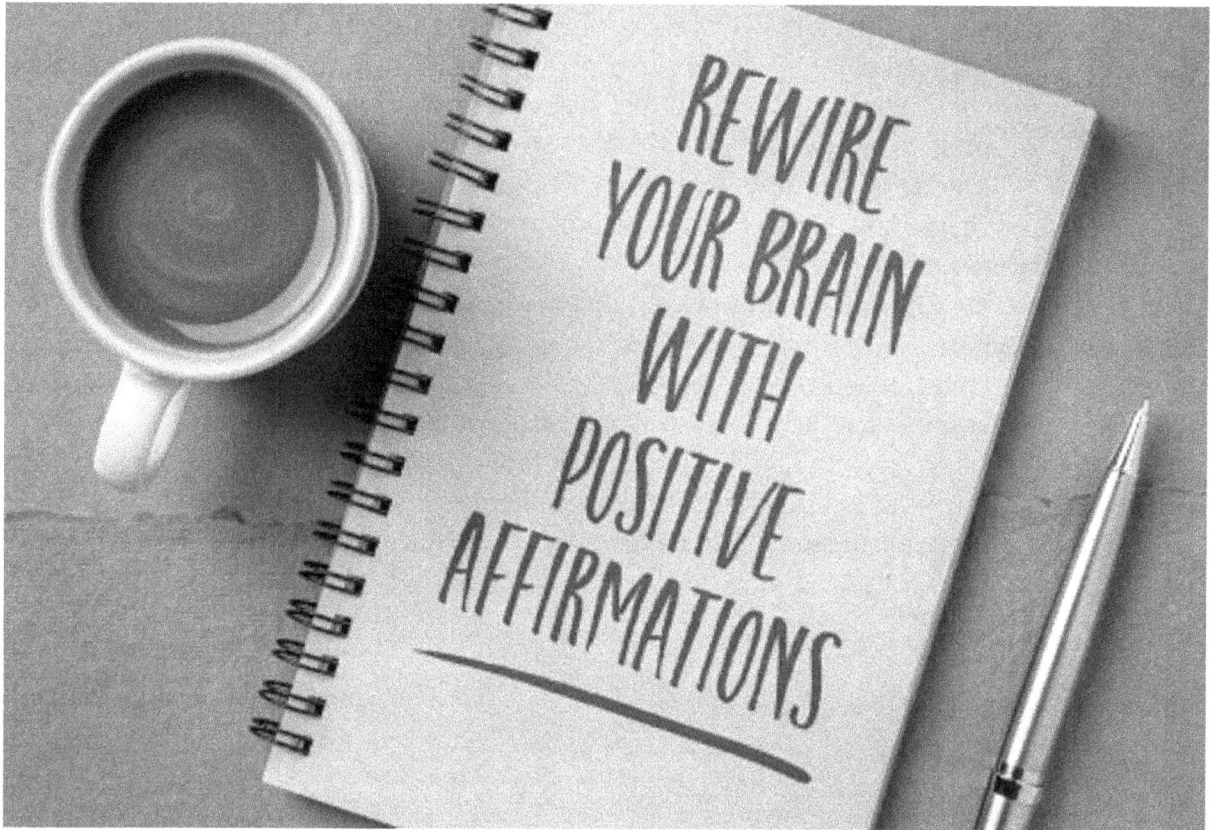

It is critical to comprehend the following fact: It's not our circumstances, nor is it the way our minds are wired, that keep us from reaching our goals. It is how our brains have been programmed to think and behave. We are our own worst adversary!

Fusion of Minds

The connection of ideas to events is known as cognitive fusion. Assume you're on an elevator that stops halfway down or up. You've been trapped inside for a few minutes, and, obviously, you're beginning to fear. However, the issue is immediately resolved, and the elevator continues on its journey, safely transporting you to your destination.

Yes, it's a terrifying event, but the chances of it occurring again are quite remote.

However, the next time you enter an elevator, you will recall the incident; your brain will recall how you behaved, and you will feel panicked once again. Unless you intervene and educate your mind to behave differently, this will happen every time you enter an elevator, and it will develop a phobia over time. This is known as cognitive fusion.

The experience gets "fused" to a certain response in your brain. To put it another way, your mind creates a habit.

You now have two options. You may either avoid elevators entirely (which is not an attractive choice when you have an important job interview on the 15th level) or retrain your mind to behave differently.

You can make cognitive fusion work for you rather than against you.

When the mind begins to perceive thoughts as facts, cognitive fusion happens. In this case, it thinks that stepping inside an elevator would cause it to stall. And since you responded with anxiety and terror the first time this occurred, your brain thinks you're in danger.

It will notify you of the risk by reinitiating your sensations of dread, worry, and panic. It seems that your brain is attempting to assist you based on the information YOU provided the first time this occurred!

The mind "fuses" the notion to the event in cognitive fusion and responds, in the same manner, each time the experience is repeated. This is true for both pleasant and bad events. Assume you're at the beach and view a stunning sunset over the water. As you watch the lovely hues stretch over the horizon and disappear, you get a sense of surprise, delight, and tranquility. The sunset is seen by your brain as a pleasant experience that makes you feel good, and it will elicit the same sensations each time you view one until they become fused to the event.

Can you see how we may unintentionally educate our brains to damage and impede rather than help? On the other hand, we may teach our brains to assist rather than hinder. Realizing that we can rewire our minds to behave in the manner we desire is a life-changing realization.

Let's continue our investigation of the brain a little further.

Two Anxiety Pathways: The Cortex and the Amygdala

Why do we feel anxious and worried?

The human brain is the only one with the capacity to envision the future. This is something no other living being can accomplish (which may be a benefit in disguise!). However, many of us, particularly when under stress, prefer to imagine negative rather than optimistic scenarios. As a consequence, we experience anxiety or worry. Again, we educate our brains to interpret the future as bad or dangerous, which leads to unpleasant thoughts and feelings.

The cerebral cortex and the Amygdala are two "anxiety pathways" in the brain that produce anxiety. They are placed in separate parts of the brain, yet they serve the same purpose.

Amygdala

This is a cluster of neurons in the form of an almond that is located deep inside the temporal lobe. It is in charge of processing survival-related thoughts and emotions such as fear, anger, pleasure, and worry. It also influences where memories are kept in the brain depending on the intensity and kind of emotions involved in the memory-creating event.

The Amygdala cannot distinguish between real

occurrences and ideas, and it reacts to both in the same manner. For example, if you are in true danger, the "fear and flight" reaction will kick in to assist you in fleeing or fighting the situation. Similarly, if you 'believe' a situation is threatening when it is not, the Amygdala will activate the same fear and flight reaction.

Cerebral Cortex

The cerebral cortex is a relatively thin layer that covers the cerebrum and ranges in thickness from 1.5 to 5 mm. It is usually referred to as "grey matter" because the nerves are not insulated, giving it a grey appearance, in contrast to the other sections of the brain, which are white. It is in charge of various processes, including personality and intelligence determination, organizational planning, language processing, sensory functions, and motor functions. The cortex also assists us in experiencing and interacting with our surroundings.

When we are in certain circumstances, our mind rushes ahead and imagines a terrible result, and this is an example of cortex-based worry. Assume you get a phone call from someone you haven't heard from in a long time. You automatically assume that the caller has terrible news, such as a death in the family, and you get concerned and nervous. Instead, the caller is inviting you to a wedding.

This is how the brain generates anxiety.

Managing the Cortex and Amygdala

Simply by managing your ideas, you may regulate the unpleasant emotions caused by the cortex and Amygdala. Remember that your mind is not the villain; it is just reacting to the things you feed it. Psychologists that specialize in this area encourage us to confront and question our ideas. Is it true that the elevator will stall every time you enter it? Is it truly possible that it will happen again? Most likely not. As a result, the terror and dread are unreasonable. Pessimists, in particular, must do so and recognize that their views do not and cannot affect the future. Exchanging negative ideas for positive ones may not change the future, but having a good attitude will make your life so much better!

Restructuring of the Mind

The first step in rewiring your mind is to take a step back and notice a specific notion. Do not strive to drive it away, but also do not surrender to it or believe it. Simply recognize the notion. Then, challenge the concept by questioning it. What proof do you have that this will occur? How probable is it to occur? Are you certain that this will be the outcome? Is it reasonable to expect this to be the case?

The process of learning to be wary of negative ideas and to develop opposing beliefs is known as cognitive restructuring.

Begin with your most repeated anxious and fearful thoughts.

Observe, recognize, and question them. Then, substitute more realistic notions for them. Doing this frequently will actually begin the metamorphosis process - the wiring of your mind will begin to alter!

Let me provide an example to demonstrate this. When you get a utility bill, you become apprehensive and concerned. You're on a limited budget and are concerned that the price would be too high.

What if you can't afford it? What if you can't afford to pay for the next one? The bills will continue to pile up until your power is turned off. You build yourself up into a panic before even opening the bill!

Instead, start the constructive reorganization process by performing the following: Take a step back from your first assumption that the cost would be too expensive. Take note of and appreciate the notion...

It causes you to be concerned and apprehensive. Now, call the notion into question. Is it appropriate to get so agitated about an energy bill? How do I know it's going to be much more than what I'm used to paying? Isn't it true that I've always managed to pay my payments on time? If the worst happens, I can borrow the money or take it from my savings, can't I? What's the big deal about it? When you continue this procedure over and again, you will eventually get that utility bill, and your mind will think, " "It's the utility bill, h. OK..." You're not exactly ecstatic, but you're also not frightened or concerned. This is something you can do with any repeated negative thinking.

What Exactly Is Self-Awareness?

First and foremost, you should understand what self-awareness is. It is being in sync with our inner world and understanding our feelings and ideas as they arise.

However, self-awareness entails much more than merely being aware of what you're thinking and experiencing. It is equally important to be able to absorb and cope with such information constructively. It is about utilizing your knowledge to manage and adjust your thoughts and emotions so that they correspond to the kind of person you want to become the circumstance you're in, and the objectives you've set for yourself.

Knowing your own strengths and flaws, your motivations, what makes you happy, what you want to change about yourself or your life, how others see you, and your views and values are all examples of self-awareness.

Your emotions and ideas.
Self-awareness is a prerequisite for every kind of personal growth or development. To be able to alter anything in your inner world, you must first be aware of what is going on in it.

If you are unconscious of your ideas, emotions, and beliefs, you will stay static, never really evolving or developing in any meaningful manner.

Self-Consciousness and Self-Esteem
At first look, it may seem that being more conscious of your inner world can only lead to a decrease in your self-esteem. After all, being acutely aware of your thoughts and emotions may just help to reinforce your negative views and attitudes about yourself. Though it may produce some uncomfortable sensations at first, gaining self-awareness does not end with wallowing in those negative feelings.

Increasing your self-awareness pushes you past them,

allowing you to build an impartial and realistic image of yourself.

There is a significant distinction between self-awareness and self-consciousness.

Self-consciousness is absorbed by your own thoughts and emotions, which you continuously analyze critically and judge yourself for. Women often suffer from self-consciousness because society has taught us that we must appear and act a particular way. When a woman does not conform to that paradigm, it is easy for her to become highly self-critical and self-conscious, always worrying about what other people think of her.

You may relax a bit if you're terrified of this concept of self-awareness because you believe it will force you to evaluate yourself too harshly. Self-awareness is the process of obtaining an objective perception of oneself. It is about acknowledging both your strengths and your limitations in order to maximize your strengths and progress in your areas of weakness. It is not, however, about being critical of one.

Someone who is self-conscious, for example, may say to them, "I'm such a dull, dumb person!" I couldn't think of a single decent suggestion throughout the meeting." Someone who is self-aware, on the other hand, could say,

"I didn't really have much to offer during this meeting, and that's OK." "Do you think I should bring a few prepared ideas next time, so I don't have to think of anything on the spur of the moment?"

Can you tell the difference? The self-conscious individual grows irritated with themselves, accusing them of being foolish and dull. The self-aware individual admits that they were unable to generate ideas on the moment and forgives themselves for this, then attempts to discover a practical way to do better in the next meeting.

Increasing your self-awareness will not reduce your self-esteem. In fact, you'll be more prepared to boost your self-esteem because you'll have an objective and true image of yourself to rely on when you start to feel like you don't measure up. But how can you cultivate a feeling of self-awareness?

5 Ways to Increase Self-Awareness

Allow yourself some breathing room.

When you're surrounded by others, it's tough to get into the habit of concentrating on your own thoughts and emotions. The cacophony and societal expectations make it difficult to just sit and listen to oneself. So, set aside sometime each day to sit quietly with yourself. It doesn't have to take a long time—just five minutes a day is a good place to start. Avoid distractions and spend a few minutes alone with your thoughts before getting up in the morning or going to bed at night.

Mindfulness should be practiced.

You might practice focused, deliberate mindfulness as you sit with your own thoughts for a few minutes. Practicing mindfulness can help you pay attention to the ideas that come rather than allowing your mind to wander and simply sort of be there.

If you choose, you may achieve this via meditation. There are several tools available to help you get started with meditation, including smartphone applications like Headspace or Calm.

Every day, keep a journal for self-reflection.

Journaling is an excellent technique to practice paying attention to your ideas.

You may just sit down with a pen and paper and jot down your thoughts and emotions from the day. Because your diary is not intended for the eyes of others, you may be as fragmented and all-over-the-place as you need to be.

You should also spend some time reflecting on your day's triumphs and shortcomings, as well as how you may be better for the following day. Keeping a journal of your self-reflection is an excellent approach to practice being nonjudgmental of yourself and identifying answers to the errors you make during the day.

Listen to others to understand their points of view.

Understanding how others view you is a component of self-awareness. So, take the time to actually listen to some trustworthy individuals about their perceptions of your strengths and flaws. Of course, you must be cautious about whoever you listen to. Some individuals may attempt to sugarcoat something you need to work on, while others may be harsh or even cruel. Being vulnerable in this way is hazardous, but it will be well worth it if you choose to listen to individuals who will be objective, honest, and compassionate.

Try out a few personality tests.

Taking a few reliable and known personality tests is a simple approach to obtain some pretty valuable information about yourself. The Myers-Briggs Type Indicator and the Enneagram Type Indicator are two examples. The official exams will cost a little money, but there are excellent free ones accessible.

Reflect

Describe the difference between self-awareness and self-consciousness in your own words.

How self-aware do you consider yourself to be?

What is one thing you could do right now to improve your self-awareness?

Chapter 12

How To Overcome Panic Thoughts

We investigated a number of elements that lead to anxiety and panic episodes. We examined anger and negativity as well as other variables that lead to anxiety and panic attacks. This chapter will concentrate on the best techniques to cope with anxiety and panic episodes. If you've been dealing with anxiety and panic attacks, you should be prepared to transition from one stage of your life to the next.

Having said that, it is crucial to emphasize that recovery from anxiety is dependent on own efforts. All of the information and guidelines in this book will only serve to open your eyes. The majority of the work must be done by you as an individual. If you want to live a life free of panic attacks and anxiety, you must remain committed to the cause.

Self-Awareness and Self-Discovery

The process of establishing whether or not you have a condition is referred to as self-discovery and awareness. It may be difficult for patients to determine if they are suffering from anxiety or panic episodes. You may never take action if you are unaware that you are suffering from anxiety. Understanding that you are a victim, on the other hand, gives you the motivation to deal with the problem firsthand.

- Step 1: Begin tracking your emotions.

Monitoring your sensations is a wonderful approach to becoming more aware of your surroundings. Self-awareness can assist you in determining how you feel about various persons or situations. If you can classify your sensations and identify every part of your surroundings that causes worry, you will be well on your way to avoiding panic attacks. It is critical to have a firm grasp of your sentiments and emotions.

This is the first stage in the process of self-discovery. You simply need to start paying attention to your emotions in this initial phase. You may, for example, opt to do a week of self-evaluation. Keep an eye on your activities when you get to work. Think about the consequences of your actions before you do them, and attempt to comprehend the role that your emotions play in every action you perform. Doing this for a week will alert your senses and make you more aware of your moods and surroundings.

- Step 2: Make a record of your emotions and activities.

The next stage is to document your emotions and activities. This phase is especially crucial for those who struggle to keep track of their emotions. If you've tried tracking your emotions but keep losing track, writing them down can be a good idea. Set your phone reminder to ring every 2 hours on a regular workday. During this time, make a list of all the key choices you've made and how they've been impacted by your emotions. Make a mental note of your mood and sentiments, as well as the repercussions of your actions.

Review your sentiments in connection to your activities at the end of the day.

Make a list of all the good and bad results. Repeat this activity for around two weeks, and you will see that low feelings lead to poor choices. You are more inclined to make bad judgments when you are angry or upset. Learning about your decision-making weaknesses can assist you in avoiding making similar terrible judgments in the future. You will begin to comprehend your moods and feelings, and as a result, you will begin to make sound judgments that are not swayed by fleeting emotions.

- Step 3: Connect your emotions, behaviors, and outcomes.

After you've written out all of your sentiments and consequences, connect them. You may even contrast the good and bad judgments you made while you were in a foul mood. This should help you learn to make choices without being influenced by your emotions. A lot of things may go wrong when you include emotions in your decision-making process. When making major life choices that may affect your work or family life, you must have a clear head.

Self-acceptance and Self-Love

Acceptance and self-love are two more ways to cope with panic attacks.

Most individuals wallow in worry because they believe they are unloved or are being targeted by others who despise them.

All of this is an illusion caused by a lack of self-love. If you want to get the love you want from the world, you must first love yourself. Self-love provides you the confidence to confront people who despise you or who criticize your decisions.

Acceptance and self-love are critical components that will assist you in tuning your mind to the realities of life. If you've been experiencing negative thoughts, you'll need to get rid of them if you want to free your mind of anxiousness. If you have been holding bad feelings like wrath and hatred, you must purge your thoughts of them in order to appreciate your life. Acceptance and self-love are required for all elements of mind purification.

Acceptance implies that you choose to accept your flaws.

Many individuals live in denial of their own shortcomings. Loss, rejection, and betrayal have all been identified as sources of negativity. Such things might cause you to experience emotional distress. Acceptance is the only method to transcend the negativity linked with hard emotional conditions.

If something awful has occurred, you must acknowledge that it has occurred. If you have lost someone or something, you must acknowledge that the loss has occurred.

Trying to argue with facts will not assist you at all.

Maintaining a state of denial might be detrimental to your mental health. You must examine all of the facts objectively to see whether there is a route back. You may attempt to recoup your losses if you believe you can do so.

However, if you see that your life is already out of control, do not attempt to force things to operate in a specific manner. Trying to make things function according to your tastes will just add to your stress. You must realize that there will be moments when you win and times when you lose in life.

Accept that there will be times when you earn a profit and others when you lose money. Trying to present yourself to the world as a flawless human will harm you more than anybody else. Do not strive to stick out or show the world that you are too powerful. Accept and move forward from tough conditions.

They are moving ahead after acceptance is infused with self-love. You can't go forward if you can't love yourself. It is frequently difficult for individuals to go on with their lives after experiencing abuse or failure. Most individuals will attempt to stick around and try to make things work. For example, if you are rejected by a romantic partner, do not strive to remain and hope that things will work out.

Do not ask someone to accept your love if they have openly rejected it. Demonstrate your affection for yourself.

Lack of acceptance and self-love often results in:

Self-esteem issues: You will lose faith in yourself if you pay too much attention to emotional abuse, loss, failure, rejection, and betrayal. All of these unpleasant emotional experiences may make you feel like a failure in life as if you do not deserve to enjoy a nice life. However, if you choose to accept your condition and choose in your mind to love yourself regardless of the circumstances, you will emerge from any scenario stronger than when you entered it.

Comparison: If you feel inadequate, it is because you have been comparing yourself to others. Comparison is an outcome of denial. If you start looking at yourself with the expectation that you should be on the same level as the other person, you may develop hate for yourself. This will result in poor self-esteem, and you may begin to blame yourself and others for your failures as a consequence.

A lack of trust will undoubtedly result from low self-esteem and shifting blame. You will begin to believe that everyone around you is mocking your activities.

You begin to see friends as adversaries, and as a consequence, you may have sadness, anxiety, panic attacks, and other mental problems.

Meditation

Meditation is another method for coping with anxiety and panic attacks. There are several meditation methods that may be utilized to enhance your moods, thoughts, and overall social life. For the sake of this book, we shall only look at two kinds of meditation: Meditation promotes mindfulness and calm.

Meditation is a practice in which you choose to concentrate your thoughts on a certain aspect of your life. When a person meditates, the mind is engaged in a visioning process. Meditation assists the practitioner in enclosing herself in a secure environment. It pulls you away from the reality that is causing you anguish and puts you in a world where you feel at ease.

Meditation is a centuries-old method that has been used for many years. Meditation was employed for medicinal reasons long before our own period. Meditation may be used to treat both emotional and physical pain. When a person meditates, the mind is altered and assisted in the release of key chemicals that are necessary for the relaxation and proper functioning of bodily organs. Meditation also improves blood flow in the body, enabling your body to be fully metabolic.

Mindfulness is a meditation practice in which the practitioner focuses only on oneself. For example, if you are the one doing the meditation, you must concentrate on yourself. Mindful meditation is a broad topic. When concentrating on yourself, you may choose to concentrate on your thoughts, physical body parts, painful locations, emotions, or any other aspect of your body. This implies that you must devote a significant amount of time to mastering mindfulness meditation. For novices, it is recommended that you concentrate on your breath or shut your eyes and concentrate on your blood flow.

Mindfulness meditation is simple.

- Step 1: Locate the ideal location.

Mindfulness meditation, like all other styles of meditation, should be practiced in a peaceful and quiet environment. To begin, look for a peaceful and quiet spot. The meditation session should last between 10 and 1 hour. Ensure that your serene place will stay silent for an extended period of time, depending on the duration of your session.

When you are in the midst of your concentration, you do not want visitors to enter.

- Step 2: Gather all of the necessary materials.

During your meditation, you will need a few items. The only thing you need for mindfulness meditation is a meditation mat or a chair. If you do decide to use a chair, make sure it has a straight back.

- Step 3: Take a position.

When you're ready to begin your meditation, choose the appropriate posture. When the practitioner sits erect, he or she is practicing mindfulness. You may sit on your mat with your legs crossed in front of you and your arms on your laps, or you can sit upright in your chair. Step 4: Close your eyes and concentrate on your breath to ensure that you are comfortable and that you can breathe freely.

With your eyes closed, concentrate on your breathing.

Feel the air enter and exit without attempting to control it. Allow your thoughts to concentrate only on your breathing until your whole attention is on your breathing. It should take you roughly 5 minutes to concentrate your attention.

If you see your mind drifting, try concentrating your attention again. For novices, it may take longer than 5 minutes to concentrate your thoughts.

- Step 5: Proceed to particular bodily sections.

You should be ready to take your awareness to the next level if you've mastered the skill of meditation by concentrating on your breath. Do not go to this level until you are certain that you can meditate by concentrating on your breath. During the first several days, you should concentrate only on your breathing. As you progress, begin concentrating on other portions of the body. At the advanced level, you may opt to concentrate on your body form. Visualize your physical form, weight, and overall alignment in your thoughts. This helps you to identify what you like and dislike about your physique.

You might alternatively opt to concentrate on your ideas. Meditation on mindfulness helps you to see your innermost aspirations. You can see what you're thinking, what you're thinking about life, and what you're thinking about love. All of these factors will help you understand who you are and why you make the decisions you make in your everyday life.

Why is mindfulness meditation beneficial for people suffering from anxiety and panic attacks?

I) Mindfulness is practiced in a judgment-free environment: The first guideline for anybody wishing to cultivate mindfulness is to be nonjudgmental. As we've seen, mindfulness may help you uncover the darkest truths about your wants. When you practice mindfulness, you will see a lot of negative aspects of yourself that you may not want to share with the rest of the world. Living a nonjudgmental life is the only way to cultivate mindfulness and be joy. People who suffer from anxiety and panic episodes tend to be judgemental. They are critical of themselves and others. Anxiety sufferers make snap judgments about individuals based on their appearance, color, or gender. They are ready to crucify individuals and designate them as dangerous or destructive. However, practicing mindfulness allows you to develop the act of being nonjudgmental.

II) Mindfulness practitioners are conscious of their own selves: Another reason individuals have anxiety and panic attacks is that they are unsure of how they feel or what they want. If you are unaware of your sentiments or wants, you may be readily triggered by events around you. Mindfulness, on the other hand, helps you to get to know oneself intimately. You learn all there is to know about your likes and wants. Nothing will surprise you if you practice mindfulness. You'll know who to avoid and how to deal with your triggers.

III) Mindfulness promotes self-acceptance: By practicing mindfulness, you learn to embrace your own strengths and faults.

This is crucial for those suffering from anxiety and panic attacks. The majority of individuals who suffer from panic attacks do not know how to love themselves. They have poor self-esteem and see themselves as weak beings. When you practice mindfulness meditation, you begin to discover your own strengths and the ability to defeat all of your adversaries.

IV) Peace and Love Meditation: Another strategy for dealing with anxiety and panic attacks is peace and love meditation. Mindfulness is not the same as peace and love meditation. Every part of your thinking revolves around your emotions and your being when you practice mindfulness. You are the fountain of peace and love to the planet when you meditate on peace and love. You must see yourself as the central component of the globe, from which love flows to the rest of the world. You concentrate on making the rest of the world happy in this form of meditation. When you are the center of peace and love, you see yourself as the one who has been entrusted with the job of making others happy. You offer love and peace to your opponents when you meditate on peace and love. Teleport yourself to a lovely planet where everyone is made to smile as a result of your affection.

How to meditate on peace and love.

- Step 1: Locate and prepare your site.

When practicing peace and love meditation, you must prepare the space in the same manner as we did for mindfulness meditation. Just make sure you choose a peaceful location and have your supplies with you. As with mindfulness meditation, you may use a chair or a mat.

- Step 2: Take a position and concentrate your mind.

You'll also need to arrange yourself on the mat or chair in the same way you did for the attentive technique. Make sure you're sitting or lying down on your mat or chair in an upright posture. Now, shut your eyes and concentrate on your breathing. This will allow you to concentrate on your ideas. Simply breathe regularly for roughly 5 minutes, keeping your thoughts focused on your breath. After 5 minutes, shift your attention from your breathing to the darkness. There should be a cloud of blackness in front of you if you shut your eyes. Simply shut your eyes and concentrate on the darkness. For around 5 minutes, focus on nothing else than the darkness.

- Step 3: Concentrate on your opponents and show them affection.

In this phase, you must choose one person who you consider to be your adversary.

Concentrate on that individual and choose to love them. Consider yourself to be the source of pleasure for your adversary. Speak to your adversary in the kindest tone you can muster in your thoughts. You may reason with your adversary and even offer them presents.

You must see yourself as a source of love. Be the one who pours love out into the world and teaches others how to love. Simply smile at your adversary and show them that life is lovely.

Chapter 13

Conversational Skills Tips to have a conversation

Make light conversation.

Sociologists have a theory that says the easiest approach to have a fluid discussion is to follow one simple rule: 30 percent talking and 70 percent listening. This is a broad guideline, and it will definitely vary depending on the scenario, so keep that in mind. However, in general, this will make you a fascinating person to speak to since you will pay attention and ask pertinent and detailed questions. This will eventually make you an attractive person to chat with.

Don't forget to introduce yourself at the conclusion of a chat.

This is only appropriate for first-time conversations, but it is an excellent technique to guarantee that the other person knows and remembers your name. Try something like "By the way, I'm..." Most of the time, the other individual will do the same thing. Always remember people's names since it's a terrific way to create an impression. You will be more likely to speak with someone who remembers your name or anything else you told them. Furthermore, remembering their name not only makes you seem knowledgeable and intelligent, but it also shows that you were paying attention.

Invite them out for coffee.

We've already discussed this trip, but it's worth repeating.

A social event allows you to actually get to know someone in a manner that you would not be able to do in another setting. Invite them to have some coffee or to the movies. You may offer them your phone number or email address to help them organize and plan.

This offers them the option of contacting you at any moment. Don't be concerned if they don't offer you their information in return; that's perfectly OK.

There will be time for that when you've gotten to know one other. One useful method to extend your invitation is to say something like, "I have to leave, but how about we go out some time, maybe for coffee or lunch?" If you ever need to contact me, here is my phone number."

Maybe they don't have enough time to meet new people. As I already said, don't take it personally. Give your contact information to individuals who have the potential to be wonderful friends, and someone will contact you eventually.

Conversations that are boring

Congratulations, the person you spoke with phoned to ask whether the coffee invitation was still available. You've made a new acquaintance! So you both agree on a date, location, and activity. When the appointment arrives, you settle down to speak and get to know one other, but you realize that the discussion fades as soon as one of you stops talking.

No matter how hard you both try, the discussion will eventually die. Even if you return to your major love (the one you mentioned the first time), the monotony and repetition weary you both. After a time, one of you decides to call it quits and go home. You return home perplexed. What transpired? What happened the second time? Everything looked to be going swimmingly the first time.

- Abortion and other health-related issues

    - Religion (essential since many individuals consider faith as a way of life; hence, unless you both share the same religion, avoid this one at all costs) - Politics - In certain cases: Sports

    While the rest may seem self-evident, you may be thinking that sports should not be on the list. However, the reality is that many individuals take sports much too seriously and will passionately defend their colors or team. It's advisable to avoid this topic unless you're an expert on the subject.

    Other topics may be off-limits depending on the situation (for example, if you notice that your interlocutor has a handicap, don't bring it up until the issue comes up spontaneously), but in general, the list should help you avoid any complications.

    That being said, if your beliefs are anchored in certain issues (for example, you may have a strong view on abortion or current politics), be mindful that just because others have an opinion on something does not mean they necessarily want to share it.

We discussed discovering what the other person enjoys. Stop utilizing social scripts or, if feasible, avoid asking questions that society makes us believe we need to ask. This is a simple approach to disrupt the social rule or norm that could dominate over the discussion (like small chat). To do this, go out of your way to learn about that person's life: "What was the finest part of your year?"

- **"What do you do for fun?"**
- "Aside from work, what is your major goal for the day?"

According to various academics on the subject, what drives our relationships and interactions with the rest of the world is a want to feel valued, appreciated and to meet new people. This is natural, and it does not imply that we are all selfish (though if you need this too often, you may develop an egocentric mentality, so be cautious). The psychology behind this is simple: if you can make someone feel special and unique by listening to and paying attention to their thoughts, emotions, or ideas, you will become appealing to them.

When you speak to someone and want to express your gratitude, you might attempt to ask them questions to find out what they consider to be important.

When they respond, you can push their thoughts a bit farther. This is tricky: Let's assume you ask them what they like most in the world. "Carpentry" is their response. In this scenario, you may ask them why and how that specific object or activity (carpentry) is essential to them. However, this does not imply that you can push them about. Don't be too harsh on them.

Keep in mind that you're attempting to be fascinating, so avoid becoming aggressive.

Suppose you're chatting to someone at a party, attempt to give them your undivided attention. Don't chat on the phone or talk to anybody other than the person you're now speaking with.

If you devote your complete focus to one individual, they will feel significant and deserving of your attention and will work hard to deserve it. If it's a nice tale, smile; if it's a humorous story, laugh; and if it's a sad one, cry. Don't go to the restroom only to read your emails or post a photo on the internet.

People will ultimately notice and may stop speaking to you. After all, their time is valuable, so why would they waste it on someone who doesn't respect it?

Your posture also reveals your level of interest in the other individual.

People automatically pick up on body language cues that indicate whether or not others are paying attention to them. Aside from not checking your phone, here are a few more recommendations you may not be aware of:

The direction in which your toes point. Yes, it seems ridiculous, but as I previously said, this is one of those indications that we pick up on without even realizing it. If you maintain your toes pointing in the direction of the person speaking, their brains will catch up on the orientation of your feet and utilize that indication to measure attention.

If you're listening to someone talk about their experiences as a parent, keep your torso and toes pointing towards them as they speak to make them feel valued and deserving of your attention. It's a nonverbal method of expressing interest and saying, "Go ahead, I'll listen."

The triple nod indicates that you are interested. It may seem strange at first, but studies have shown that giving someone a triple nod causes them to talk two to four times longer.

This serves as a subliminal trigger to continue reading and expanding their tale.

When someone finishes speaking, and you suspect there is more to it, look them in the eyes and nod three times. Most of the time, they will continue their tale, and if they do not, you can always ask another question connected to what they have been discussing.

If you see that the discussion is coming to an end, offer open-ended inquiries.

This will assist in keeping the discussion going. Assume your interlocutor is discussing ancient Roman history, and you notice that the conversation has reached a point when neither of you knows what to say. In such a situation, pose a question that may take some time to respond completely. In the previous example, inquire about the distinctions between Romans and Greeks, as well as how one civilization adapted to the other.

Keep in mind that I'm only providing you random samples from previous discussions, and you may always ask anything you want. This will help you avoid "yes" and "no" responses, let your interlocutor express himself, and share more information with you so you can continue the discussion.

Perhaps this is the appropriate moment to bring it up,

but dialogues should not be conducted in the manner of a police interrogation. While some inquiry is acceptable, it must not be at the price of your interlocutor's tranquility. I advised expanding the topic a little further, but never to the point of making the other person feel uncomfortable. Allow them to go someplace else to chat or do something different if they don't want to answer a question.

They owe you no response, and if they don't want to talk, they have no duty to do so. During my reading and observing people interact, I've seen some uncomfortable individuals imposing their thoughts and beliefs on the rest of the group because they mistakenly felt that the major purpose of any debate is to win the argument. This is a major blunder that you should avoid at all costs.

Another way to start and maintain a conversation is to bring up something remarkable that they are wearing or something specific about the location you are both in. In the last anecdote, my friend's wife inquired about the t-shirt.

This is a great method to start a discussion since if they are wearing something distinctive, they will be more likely to chat about it. Whether they have another distinctive item of apparel, such as special earrings, it might start a debate about where they obtained them and if they got them while traveling abroad. If they don't have anything specific in mind, you may always remark on your surroundings and use it as a cue to chat about whatever comes to mind. Assume that during the party you're both attending, there are separate candles lighting up the space. In such instance, you may say something like, "They remind me of the candles my grandmother used to use" (or whatever it tells you; of all, you don't have to follow exactly what I write here!). This, in turn, will have a snowball effect in the discourse, keeping it going.

Continue to practice these stages, and you will see that with enough experience, you will find yourself talking much more in-depth than you imagined in every discussion.

But let's take a step back and look at the bad side of things: Whatever you do, the discussion dies. You did all you could, and you must recognize that you are not obligated to like everyone you encounter in your life. Some of them may form long-term relationships with you, while others will pass through your life. That's OK, and the best approach in these situations is to withdraw and go on to another individual with whom you may feel better connected or have more in common.

Continue the Conversation Getting Past the Niceties

The uncomfortable silence that many of us face after participating in a significant bit of small chat is one of the most unsettling aspects of being in a discussion, particularly with strangers.

Many people avoid engaging in conversation because of the uncomfortable silence. Now that you've mastered your fear of talking to strangers, introduced yourself in the best manner possible, and participated in a reasonable amount of small talk using conversation starters, the next task is to never run out of things to say. How do we keep the discussion going while keeping it engaging and flowing?

To address this issue, you must first understand why the uncomfortable silence occurs, particularly while chatting with strangers. The uncomfortable silence is internal because it occurs when you believe you have run out of things to say. You've turned on a filter that sifts through what you believe is appropriate to say to a stranger, restricting your options.

When you're talking with somebody you know well, this filter is essentially non-existent. You can talk for hours about unrelated issues without worrying about what to say next. When speaking to a friend or acquaintance, your "good enough for conversation" threshold is quite low. If you feel like bringing up an intriguing issue that comes to mind, you just do so.

That is the key to extending a discussion beyond the niceties. You must let go of your inhibitions and refrain from filtering things out of your speech. If a subject or notion is excellent enough to be spoken about, do so. You must learn to adjust to on-the-fly talks, which you may achieve by eliminating this filter.

You must be emotionally exposed in order to keep the discussion moving beyond small chats and niceties. This does not imply that you must share your deepest darkest secret. All it implies is that you must take the initiative by opening up first. Be the first to advance the discussion beyond niceties by sharing a personal story. Here's why this is significant.

When you pay attention, you will learn a few things about the other person. Even so, you should not approach a stranger and urge him or her to reveal his or her innermost secrets. After all, you wouldn't expect someone you just met to ask you the same question. When you are vulnerable and disclose something about yourself with the other person first, you are more likely to be trusted.

People respond in kind when they feel trustworthy. Because you've given yourself up to them, they'll open up to you, which will deepen the dialogue.

Discover How to Turn Strangers Into Friends.

The best things in life come to those who are ready to risk rejection and failure. The fear of rejection is exactly what has been preventing you from forming long-lasting friendships and interactions with strangers. You have conquered this fear now that you have completed stages 1 through 5. Congratulations! You are now prepared to take on the task of converting a random discussion with a stranger into a long-lasting friendship. Here's how to do it:

Make the most of your similarities.

At this stage, we'll presume that the stranger you want to make a friend with is someone you've had a small chat with and concluded is someone worth becoming a friend with after developing the discussion, matching, and mirroring.

You may build on similarities to keep this dialogue continuing and your connection developing. For example, if both you and the stranger/acquaintance like hiking and you and many other friends have scheduled a walk in the future weeks or months, you may casually invite this person and then continue developing the discussion on this common ground. Because the individual enjoys hiking, he or she is more likely to say yes, giving you the opportunity to see the person again. This next contact will solidify the acquaintance and transform it into a blossoming relationship.

Don't Forget to Include Your Contact Information.

Before you go your own ways after having a terrific first discussion with someone you just met, read the circumstances. Take the initiative and ask for contact information if you believe the individual had a good time chatting with you (particularly if, as in the previous example, the person agrees to come for the scheduled hike).

Having your "new friend's" contact information can make communication simpler when you decide to meet up again. When it comes to requesting contact information, be straightforward. "I had so much joy conversing with you," you may say. Before you go, let's exchange phone numbers so we can meet up and talk more about that trek."

Be Approachable

We have said on several occasions that acquaintances are more drawn to us and hence more receptive to friendships if we are honest and vulnerable on a personal level. This is what we mean when we say we're friendly.

Once you've completed stages 1-5 of connecting with a stranger, that person is no longer a stranger; instead, he or she is an acquaintance, which is a step closer to friendship. Treat such a person like you would a friend, which means you should establish an atmosphere of open communication and familiarity while discussing and acting on similar interests.

Conclusion

Dealing with the truths regarding borderline personality disorder is something no one wants to do. It may be difficult for everyone concerned. An individual suffering from this disease is acting out and behaving in the manner they believe they should since it is the only thing they know how to do. On the other side, the conduct will make no sense to the person's family and friends since they are the ones who are being damaged in the process. Feelings may be hurt on either side, but after reading this handbook, it is simpler to understand why the person with this disease has been acting out for so long.

This is a complex condition that should not be handled lightly. Individual who has been suffering from this disease will need all of the assistance and support that they can obtain in order to fully heal. It is not a simple task since many of the chemicals and ideas in their own brain are affecting the behavior that is there. However, therapy is the only way to provide them the assistance they need to feel better and return to their regular lives with their friends and family.

Friends and relatives may help the person with a borderline personality disorder by volunteering to be supportive and present while they are in treatment. They may also seek to get some of their own counseling to ensure that they are doing well throughout the process. This is difficult for both of you, but blaming your loved one will make the situation much more difficult to cope with. Being together is the most effective method for everyone to get through this.

Understanding what is causing this issue is often the first step. Most families who learn that a loved one has this personality disorder get even more disturbed or angry at the individual than they were before the diagnosis. This is often due to a lack of understanding of the disease, leading them to believe that the person is lying to them, concealing something, or that nothing is wrong with them. Not only is the family to blame, but the individual with the condition may be feeling the same way, which is why they may be so resistant to receiving the care they need.

This manual is intended to provide much of the information that persons suffering from the condition, as well as their family members and friends, will need to get through this difficult period. The individual is often attempting to overcome a distressing event from their upbringing, which is not always as simple as others may believe.

It may take a long time, possibly years or more, to figure it out, but with the correct knowledge and support, they will be OK. In reality, the majority of people who receive the therapy they need and continue with it are able to return to a normal life with their family and friends, and they will never relapse again.

Use this manual to get a head start in understanding this illness. There's a lot to it, and it's easy to confuse borderline personality disorder with one of the other illnesses out there. This manual attempted to clear up some of the myths so that it is simpler to comprehend what is going on and how the suffering might be most effectively supported. If you or someone you know is suffering from this disease, it is critical that they get the necessary treatment as soon as possible. Using this manual is one of the finest methods to assist them and return them to the life they deserve.

www.ingramcontent.com/pod-product-compliance
Lightning Source LLC
Chambersburg PA
CBHW080622030426
42336CB00018B/3047